MAKE THIS
YOUR LUCKY DAY

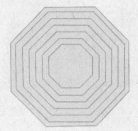

MAKE THIS
YOUR LUCKY DAY

Fun and Easy Feng Shui Secrets to Success,
Romance, Health, and Harmony

ELLEN WHITEHURST

BALLANTINE BOOKS 🏛 NEW YORK

A Ballantine Books Trade Paperback Original

Published in the United States by Ballantine Books,
an imprint of The Random House Publishing Group,
a division of Random House, Inc., New York.

Library of Congress Cataloging-in-Publication Data

Whitehurst, Ellen.
Make this your lucky day : fun and easy Feng Shui secrets to
success, romance, health, and harmony / Ellen Whitehurst.
p.   cm.
ISBN 978-0-345-50054-0 (pbk.)
1. Feng shui.   I. Title.

BF1779.F4W55 2008
133.3'337—dc22   2007028734

Printed in the United States of America

www.ballantinebooks.com

246897531

Book design by Jo Anne Metsch

To the light of my life,

who makes every day *my* lucky day

—to my son, Grayson, with love.

To the person who filled this book with love and light,

thereby making all of our lives luckier and more fortunate

—to Billie with my love and my thanks.

To Grandmaster Lin Yun,

who fills the entire planet with love and light,

my unending gratitude and thanks.

CONTENTS

INTRODUCTION

WHAT IF I told you that there really is a way to find your soul mate, get your dream job with your dream salary, enable your kids to get the best possible grades, and achieve optimal health? What if I told you that you can make sure a first date goes on to a second and third, marry your soul mate, and then get pregnant (if that is your wish)? Or, if your emphasis is on your job, what if I told you that you can enhance any aspect of your career, increase your income, and build your bottom line all at once, in an easy and fun fashion?

What if I told you, no, promised you, that there is a magic wand that you can wave across every aspect of your life to make it happier, healthier, and more prosperous, and that the wand is nestled in your hands right now?

Make This Your Lucky Day is that magic wand. It is a book of secrets and shortcuts that will enable you to make each day of your life luckier. Within these pages I offer hundreds of tips and techniques that have the power to enhance the quality of your life, change its fortune, and bring you luck. This book is the loving result of many years of passionate training, thousands of client consultations, and even more hours of helping people access their best selves in order to live their best lives.

In the strictest terms, I am a Feng Shui practitioner, but I have also delved into many other modalities, all focused on enhancing one's life. My extensive work in alternative healing and lifestyles has enabled me to infuse my special brand of cures and adjustments with the ancient richness of traditional Feng Shui advice, as well as additional secrets from other rich and varied traditions, including Native American, Buddhism, Judaism, along with some African cultures, to name just a few.

For this reason, *Make This Your Lucky Day* is not a typical Feng Shui book. Not at all. Although I have extensive training in this ancient field, I have created a special brand of Lucky Day Shui that includes and exceeds Feng Shui, so that the cures offered in this book are "fast, fun, and easy"—that phrase captures both my brand of Feng Shui and my personality to a tee! I want people to be able to tap into these cures NOW so that they see the positive, life-enhancing results quickly and concretely.

Although the essence of Feng Shui is both scientific and philosophical in nature, its practical application is very much rooted in what works to make life more livable in the here and now. Feng Shui posits that everything you place in the environment around you reflects what's going on inside you. But many people make the mistaken assumption that Feng Shui is about moving furniture. Not true. It's much more than that, and can be much less complicated. I believe that Feng Shui creates and constitutes harmonious relationships between your interior self and your exterior atmosphere. This harmonic ordering of space can influence every area of your life while it contributes to your happiness, wealth, and good health.

However, what's distinct and unique about *Make This Your Lucky Day* is that instead of finding general ways to enhance these areas of your life, you will find very specific cures targeted to special days, milestones, and life situations. This way, you can

go to the Contents pages, find what day or event is of importance to you now, and then access those cures to enhance that
celebratory day, make that special event (a birthday, an anniversary, the birth of a child) even more special, or give a boost of
support to a significant life situation (first day of a new job,
dream date, moving day, or loss of a loved one). I've purposely
made these cures fast, fun, and easy so that you can do them
quickly and reap the benefits immediately. All of the cures are
meant to inspire, create, and encourage the Three Great Blessings
of Feng Shui—Health, Happiness, and Prosperity—to come in
and sit awhile in your personal space on special days, or any day
that you feel you need some extra luck. They will make special
days more special, but more than that they will make every day
your lucky day.

Some of these days fall neatly on the calendar, highlighted as
holidays, including New Year's Day, Valentine's Day, Presidents'
Day, Easter, Passover, Fourth of July, Halloween, Thanksgiving,
Christmas, and more. But in addition to these more obvious special days, I have also included those days in our lives that are
milestones—such as the day your child is born, the first day of
school, or your first day at a new job. The sections Dream Date,
Stories to (Get and) Keep You Engaged, and Wedding Day Shui
offer advice that will help you focus and enhance your love life,
while topics such as I'm (Finally!!!)! Pregnant, Itty-Bitty Baby
Shui, Christening or Baby-Naming, and First Day of School
Shui, can help you increase your fertility and enhance the lives
and fortunes of your children—from the very first moment they
are conceived!

Within these special days, events, and life situations, you will
learn amazing adjustments that will empower your career, your
personal goals and dreams, and your ability to receive the recognition you've earned in your life. Are you interested in knowing

how to enhance your impression on the first day of a new job? Do you want to know how to increase your chances of getting a raise, the healthy one you know you deserve? What about advice on how to get a leg up on the competition, literally, if you are involved in any kind of competitive sports event? You will learn cures to get you out of debt, help offset the stress of tax day, and increase your financial largesse across the board. If you want it, I will tell you how to get it, and how to get it now, no matter what it is.

You will gain insight and advice on how to smooth all your relationships with family and friends, whether they're old, new, or dearly departed. Special cures will strengthen your bond with your mother and your father, and even give you quick ways to resolve discord in these relationships. You will learn how to honor your grandparents so that you can protect your family tree, and should you be facing the death of a loved one, you will find ways to find more succor and support. By pulling on the power of mentors and guides, you will also learn how to make all in your life run more smoothly.

So if you're moving into a new home, traveling on vacation or business, or are looking for advice on how to best weather the end of a relationship, or any other life passage, you will be able to find cures and adjustments based on that day, or that particular circumstance or challenge, to support and guide you.

I've also included fun and useful sidebars throughout the book that are filled with enticing recipes, delightful decorating ideas, and other lifestyle tips to further reinforce the cures offered for the special days that will add so much more luck to your life.

Indeed, it is my promise to you that I can show you how you can enhance all the aspects of your life—from love and romance to finances to children to your health—and the list goes on—

and to do all of this in bite-sized, easy-to-swallow, palatable pieces. I know this, I believe this, and I've seen these cures and adjustments work over and over and over again.

I have presented these cures using what's called, in Western Feng Shui, the Bagua, which is a nine-sectored navigational map that corresponds to different areas or energies that each of us will experience at some point in our lives (see page xxiv). Feng Shui's main tool contains nine sectors, or *guas,* that correspond to all the areas of your life—Career (your sense of self-worth or self-esteem), Knowledge and Self-Cultivation (how well you show yourself that you can love yourself, with a lot of wisdom thrown in for good measure), Family, Friends, and Ancestors (well, pretty much exactly what it says, your family tree), Wealth and Prosperity (abundance, joy, receiving all you deserve), Fame and Reputation (being rewarded and recognized for all the things you do, from folding the laundry to writing software applications for Apple's newest iPod), Relationship, Romance, and Marriage (love, romance, and everyday relationships), Children and Creativity (from the one cooing at your breast to the babies bounding around in your head that can make you your next million), Helpful People and Travel (trips and life travels you'd like to take and the instrumental people who can help you get there), and, finally, Health (on the physical, emotional, mental, and spiritual levels).

Again, the cures and adjustments of my brand of Feng Shui act quickly and are incredibly easy to implement. As I've been heard to say a time or two, "You really don't have to spend ten years on the couch; sometimes you just have to move it." My company tagline reads "Secrets and Shortcuts to Fast Fortune and Luck." For me, that about says it all. Well, that and how tremendously fortunate I am that I can share these techniques with all of you who want to improve any piece or part of your own life or those of your loved ones. As I have also been heard to say (a few thousand or more times), "Who can't use a little more luck?" I, for one, absolutely know the answer is, "Whoever wants it, whenever they want it," because it's all here, in this book in your hands right now.

WHY I *HAD* TO WRITE THIS BOOK

Before we get to all the easy and wonderful ways you can make YOUR life a lot luckier and much more fortune-filled, as well as more enjoyable and satisfying, I'd like to share with you a bit about my own interesting life and how this book came to be. Like many people who have radically changed their careers, for whatever reason, I've carved my own path down a road slightly less traveled. I began my career on Wall Street, only to find myself a number of years later in the extremely different, almost diametrically opposed world of holistic health, alternative life-styles, and Feng Shui—quite a departure from the blue-and-gray-suit brigade. At the time, I was an assistant manager in the Commodity News Department of the now defunct (remember how everyone was "listening" to) E. F. Hutton and rose steadily through the ranks as one of few twenty-something professional women, eventually trading the commodity markets for my own clients, managing, at one particular stretch, millions of dollars at a time.

During this period, I met and married a fellow commodity trader, a man who was used to taking big risks, as he did this time as well, by wedding a woman almost thirty years his junior. Little did I realize then the impact that age difference would later have on our lives. In those early days, my life was fulfilling, and, as my cronies often commented, "absolutely fabulous." Days rushed by in a whirlwind of good friends, good fortune, and lots of welcome opportunities to commit some serious acts of charity. Both my marriage and my career were healthy and wealthy, but, deep down, I constantly felt I was missing that proverbial "wise" part, you know, that certain something that makes you know why you were ever born in the first place. Some call it their "calling," some refer to it as their "life's mission"; in those days, I called it nonexistent. Although I was enjoying a lifestyle made comfortable by having houses in New York City, the east end of Long Island, Hilton Head Island, and south Florida, I just never quite felt at home with myself.

And just as all was in place and poised for continued success, the first of my unexpected but totally transforming experiences happened to shake up my oh-so-stable and secure life. My father's lifelong struggle with diabetes had suddenly progressed significantly, and my mother's breast cancer had dramatically come out of remission, so dramatically that on Tuesday she was fine and on Wednesday she was dying. So began a period in which I watched helplessly as my parents struggled daily in the face of their debilitating diseases and woefully insufficient pain management. Each day they faced inordinate pain, while I stood by with my family, wondering what in the world we could do to help them. As my parents' conditions worsened, and they almost concurrently passed into morphine-dependent states, I frantically began investigating and researching alternative ways to relieve their suffering, as well as the rest of my family's emotional stress. I started taking classes and got licensed in a modality called phytoaromatology (the use of essential oils for medicinal treatments). I consulted acupuncturists and osteopaths, delved into meditation and herbalism, researched ways that vitamins could be used for healing, and explored Feng Shui. I brought all these ideas to my parents with the hope that they would try something—anything—to relieve their constant discomfort and improve—even fractionally—their rapidly declining quality of life.

This was some years ago, and many of these holistic health techniques or practices had not yet reached mainstream America; they certainly had not been integrated into Western medical treatments. So my fighting Irish parents, steeped in their own orthodoxy, were not about to try any of my "woo-woo" suggestions for alleviating their precipitous declines. However, compelled as both a daughter and a human being, I continued to pursue knowledge in the area of holistic health and healing—if it wasn't my parents I could help, then it would have to be someone else. And in the back of my mind I began to realize something: That empty void I'd always been feeling was slowly starting to fill, and I was getting a sense, a taste, and a glimpse of just what I'd been put on this planet to do.

I have always believed that when you're ready to learn, a teacher appears. And looking back at this time in my life, I know that the teacher of this life lesson was indeed my parents' illnesses and that my legacy was their eventual deaths. So while I mourn their loss each and every day, I am very grateful to them for the door of holistic medicine that was opened to me. Indeed, it soon offered me not just another path to pursue, but an even bigger, richer gift in return.

After both of my parents died, my husband and I more or less settled in Miami, Florida, and I began delving into Feng Shui more fully. Like a moth to a flame, I was drawn to this ancient practice and needed to know absolutely everything I could about it. I attended hundreds of lectures and symposiums. I read even more texts—both ancient and modern. And I made it a point to meet and learn from as many masters of Feng Shui and natural teachers and herbalists as I could access. I soon opened a fledgling consulting practice, working with clients one-on-one as well as in larger groups.

During this time, when I was first developing my Feng Shui practice, I offered to help a very sick friend find some peace with his father, with whom he hadn't spoken in years. When I approached Richard with a "cure" I had learned from Feng Shui, he said, "Just don't tell me I have to bite the head off a chicken and dance around the backyard naked or anything else like that!" This was a pretty typical response in those early days. I persevered and, after very little persuasion, Richard said he was willing to try to reconnect with his dad, after years of homophobic acrimony between them—just as long as there was no poultry involved.

Not intimidated by my friend's skepticism, I suggested that he enact a small Feng Shui cure: to write a letter to his father using red pen (red being one of Feng Shui's most powerful colors) saying whatever he wanted, but trying to tell his father somewhere inside the letter that he loved him—something, by the way, we all need to do all the time. I then instructed my friend to fold the letter in quarters and place it in the Family sector of his bedroom (this relates to the nine-sectored Feng Shui Bagua, or map, which you will learn about on pages xxiii–xxvii), put a healthy green plant on top of the letter (wood is the element associated with this area's energies—family tree, roots—get it?), and leave the letter there for nine days (nine being an important number, as you will soon learn). After those nine days Richard could then decide to send the letter directly to his dad, rewrite the letter, or even burn it (like sending Universal smoke signals)—either way, the message of love would reach his father.

After nine days, my friend decided to burn the letter in his kitchen sink (according to Feng Shui the kitchen sink has "clean water" and therefore is a good place for this sort of activity). Immediately after, Richard began to feel a sense of release and resolve, which was only magnified when his father "miraculously" (Richard's word) called him later that very same night at midnight. Although my dear friend died a few weeks later, he had reached a peace he had never imagined possible, and, as I could never have imagined, his father was instrumental in helping to arrange his funeral.

This was one of the first of many ways I saw people use Feng Shui and other alternative modalities to heal and enhance their lives. The beauty and power of these techniques to relieve pain and uplift the spirit was simply mind-boggling and incredibly gratifying to me. I soon realized that the ever-present void within me was indeed filling and fading, and I knew with a clear certainty that I had found my passion, my mission, and my calling: to help *you* use these ancient healing customs with a contemporary spin in order to bring divine order into your life.

This experience with my good friend Richard and with so many others gave me the courage to expand my practice. My days, months, and years were now being spent with people who had contacted me, wanting to learn my brand of self-empowerment to help cure their emotional ailments, ready their houses for sale, and make their lives and living spaces more comfortable. In general, they all wanted health and peace of mind on every conceivable level—physical, emotional, mental—and, *fortunately,* I have those answers. And as my business grew, so did the number of success stories: from the woman who found her soul mate after searching and seeking for close to fifty years to the window franchise owners who went from scratch to earning $12 million a year in under five years to the kids who wouldn't sleep through the night to the arthritis that wouldn't sleep at all—all of these "miraculous" changes being achieved with some well-placed adjustments and cures. This stuff was great and it really worked!

But, as sometimes happens, I was presented with yet another "opportunity to grow" (read: BIG challenge). I was catapulted from a life of easy luxury to one in which I was forced to make my passionate interest in Feng Shui into something that was stable and income-producing. Necessity is the mother of invention, right? But even old Tom Edison couldn't have seen what was about to happen next. In short order, my husband announced that we had lost every last dime in the bank, the Picasso painting in the living room, and the Rolls-Royce in the garage—all in a series of bad investments. We were now officially and critically crippled financially. After twenty-two years of these sorts of financial ups and downs created by the constant risks associated with playing the gambling game of commodity trading, both my marriage and my bank account were blown to smithereens. The bottom line was simple: There now was no bottom line and we were dead broke.

So, in my inimitable fashion, I went for broke, literally, and got even more serious about expanding my burgeoning business and building my lucky little brand. Although my business started out small, I had big dreams of making this start-up not only a great success but, much more important, one that would make a positive and impact-filled difference in people's lives. I wanted to share this information—not only with the hundreds whom I had been encountering in my seminars and one-on-one client visits but with the whole world. This then became my dearest desire and deepest intention, one I felt deep in my bones and which I've now written down here in this book.

The information contained in *Make This Your Lucky Day* has enriched and enhanced my own life and the lives of my thousands of clients. I now wish to extend this knowledge and insight to you so that you can enhance and enrich your life and the lives of your loved ones—especially on those days that matter most—when we can always use a little more luck, a lot more fortune, and many, many blessings—which is what I wish for you—immense amounts of fortune and luck. So please do enjoy the read and the incredible results you will receive!

HOW TO USE THIS BOOK

UNDERSTANDING THE BAGUA

The Bagua (pronounced Ba-gwa) map is a color chart with nine sectors (see illustration on page xxiv). Each sector represents a specific life situation that can be correlated with a specific energy that sits inside your home or office, or anywhere you care to address energetic anomalies. By using the Bagua to divide your space (of your home, your office, or any room in your home), you can improve your quality of life by improving that environment. Most of the cures or adjustments I offer in the pages that follow correspond to one or more areas of the Bagua map, so the more familiar you are with its layout, the faster, easier, and more fun it will be to access the secrets, learn the shortcuts, and enjoy the results. Here's how to walk your Bagua map:

1. In your mind's eye (or even on an actual blueprint) visualize the space that you are attempting to Feng Shui as a perfect square or rectangle. (DO NOT INCLUDE ANY SPACES BUILT AS ADDITIONS. These areas get Feng Shui'd separately within your personal space by using the Bagua independently.)

2. Now divide this space into nine equal squares, sort of like a tic-tac-toe board.
3. This grid is known as the Feng Shui BAGUA MAP. Use the accompanying illustration to navigate through the Bagua.
4. Align the bottom of the board, or grid, with the same wall that includes the front or formal entranceway. THIS IS THE DOOR THAT THE BUILDER INTENDED AS THE FORMAL ENTRANCE. It does not matter what door you use most often. We are speaking only of the front door.

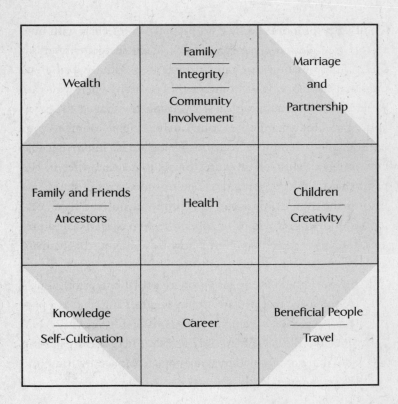

Wealth	Family ——— Integrity ——— Community Involvement	Marriage and Partnership
Family and Friends ——— Ancestors	Health	Children ——— Creativity
Knowledge ——— Self-Cultivation	Career	Beneficial People ——— Travel

5. Your entrance, then, will fall into one of the three front, or bottom, sectors (individually called *guas*) on this Feng Shui Bagua map.

6. Your entrance through the Bagua map will fall into Knowledge and Self-Cultivation or Career or Beneficial People. There are no exceptions to this. Sometimes, though, your entrance will "straddle," or "bleed," into two different areas. This is fine. Just remember to divide the main floor into nine equal spaces as if there were no standing walls in the house and it was an empty plane to work with.

7. Standing at the threshold, either facing your front door or with your back to the street side (or hallway), you are now ready to identify which locations correspond to the energies of which sector on the grid of the Bagua.

8. Although the basement, second, and third floors in the home/office should eventually be appropriately assessed, for immediate and accurate Feng Shui response, we are superimposing this Feng Shui Bagua map only onto what would be considered the main floor. You may additionally center this grid, or map, or Bagua map, over any individual room and begin to Feng Shui as the macrocosm to the micro. But I like to use the pecking order of main floor first, master bedroom second, living room third, and outside of property last.

9. You can even employ this method of superimposing this Bagua over the top of your desk using your seating as the "entryway."

10. Just be sure to remember that one of the three energetic grids that lie along the same wall as the front door will ALWAYS be your entranceway and the rest of the Feng Shui Bagua remains fixed according to that entry. For example,

if money is an issue or concern, then stand stationary at your front entrance with your back to the street (or hallway). Now, where is the far back left-hand wall located? That's right, the wall that is farthest left and to the back of the whole space, well, that's your WEALTH area of the Bagua map and you have now located it. Now make an adjustment to stimulate the Chi (the energy in your environment) and watch your fortunes become fruitful. See? Easy.

For those of you who are interested in learning more about Feng Shui, it bears keeping in mind that I was trained in the Western School Feng Shui, which is also known as Black Hat Feng Shui. If you decide to continue to pursue the study of Feng Shui, remember that thus far you have been enjoying enhancements from the Western School, which has evolved from the revered and original Eastern, or Compass, School of Feng Shui.

A NOTE TO READERS

The adjustments and cures specific to each of the special days highlighted correspond in some way to one of the nine energies associated with all the life stages represented on the Bagua map. By activating a cure, you are then able to identify potential or even existing problems, find (often immediate) solutions, and create your own luck or good fortune for that day or, really, for every day. With this book, you can focus on how to make certain special days on the calendar—or any day you wish—more memorable, smooth, joyful, and successful, which in turn will positively impact your entire life and the lives of all those around you.

As you become more accustomed to both the Bagua and how to use the cures throughout the book, you will see that some adjustments enhance more than one energy or sector of the Bagua. But keep in mind that you can pick and choose the remedies that work for you—on whatever day you want to use them! The days are not meant to limit your options but to guide how you use the cures.

Also, if one of the cures doesn't seem to resonate with you, then simply choose one that does. You will know what it is that you need because it will speak to you. And I have offered many options along the way!

You will notice, too, that often numbers and colors, along with elements, play an important part in changing your luck or fortune. People always ask about the origin and meaning behind these assignations. Sometimes the symbolism is quite clear and you can guess at its significance from a metaphorical standpoint. For instance, Wealth is associated with the element wood (grow your money) and the color purple (traditionally the color of emperors and kings). But in other cases, the colors and elements are more obscure. Suffice it to say that some of the reasons are so ancient and complex, if I were to insert all of that here, you would be reading a dry-as-dirt reference book instead of a short, sassy, and eminently practical book of cures! After spending so much of my own time and energy explaining how best to use this info, for you to achieve your best life, it's time to get started doing exactly that. Now go and make this your Lucky Day!

MAKE THIS
YOUR LUCKY DAY

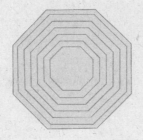

	1	
Wealth and Prosperity	Fame and Reputation	Relationship, Romance, and Marriage
Family, Friends, and Ancestors	Health	Children and Creativity
Knowledge and Self-Cultivation	**Career**	Helpful People and Travel

THE ENERGIES ASSOCIATED with this sector obviously will speak to your job, your income, and how you make a living and grab your paycheck. But it's so, so, so much more than that. This sector is about how you feel about yourself, way deep down inside. It goes directly to your sense of who you are, your self-esteem, and your confidence in your ability to take charge of your life. It's about who you are at your very core and how much you, individually, have to offer the world. See, every single solitary soul born on this planet brings with him or her something entirely special and unique to and for that person only. Gifts and talents, things that only they can do better than anyone else because those gifts and talents define their very identity and ideals as well as bring bright expectations and fuel to their dreams.

Mrs. Fields evidently can bake a better chocolate chip cookie than I can (but, to be honest, that's not very hard to do). That's her gift, her talent, and, BONUS, she loves doing it. You get it, it's the old Joseph Campbell admonition to always "follow your bliss," because if you do what you absolutely love and are good at it, then the money will naturally follow.

The harder question then remains: "What is my bliss?" "What am I better at than anyone else?" Uh-oh, is that a self-esteem issue I hear creeping into the Career area? Seriously, sometimes I have clients who have become so far removed from themselves and whatever their special gifts and talents are that I have to ask them to take a moment to answer this invasive but oh-so-illuminating question: "Okay, if I called your mother (or whoever raised you) right now, dead or alive, and asked her what you LOVED to do as a kid, what would she tell me?" Because chances are really, really high that whatever you loved to do as a kid is something shy of how you should be earning a paycheck now.

Or, we can take the more "holistic" route where I ask, "What would happen if there were no money in the world and we all had to barter with one another to exist? Obviously your neighbor Joe the plumber could fix your broken pipes, but what, then, could you possibly offer him in return?"

These are the really hard questions. In fact, they are standard Psychology 101. Why am I here? What's the point? To live, work, pay taxes, and die? NO! So, you see, although this energy has a name called Career, it's really all about YOU! Your gifts! Your talents! And your making money from them (because, let's face it, Joe ain't fixing your pipes for even anywhere close to free anytime soon). Your special gifts are there, that much I know. They sometimes get buried by the need to pay the mortgage, the tuition, the monthly telephone bill, but they exist and they are calling you nonetheless.

So, maybe someday you can stop to answer that call (and smell the roses while you're at it, especially if you have a talent for floral arranging), and give some thought to what it is you've always dreamed about doing. Then take some of the time-tested and success-filled suggestions that follow and go get yourself the job of your dreams. If that's a bit too much of a leap for you at this moment, just start thinking about what you'd love to be doing day in and day out and do something, anything, to get that party started.

In the meantime, the adjustments and cures included herein will bring you to the ladder and help you climb it, higher and higher, until you are at the tippy-top rung and ready to start all over again. And when that happens, try to give some thought to what the world would love from you. And see if you can use some of these cures to get to that place because then, my friend, you will have come home.

Career is primarily located in the bottom, or front, middle of the main floor, the living room, and especially your office, or any space you spend a lot of time in. In the tic-tac-toe-board analogy, it is the center bottom square, or sector, of your Bagua map. The element here is water and the color is black. If the energy of Career also asks "Why am I here?" then it might follow that to place water in this space represents the eternal mother, the womb, and the water from which we are all birthed. Water itself deep down is black (the only reason it appears blue to us is the reflection from the sun). So from the dark depths of the womb we emerge alone to forge our potentially perfect path. Alone. Therefore the number associated here is 1. Place one black frame here with a picture of moving water in it to create your own flow—soon you will find yourself floating in a space of personal peace and bliss.

FINDING A NEW JOB

Anyone actively searching for a new job is in so many ways about to embark on so many new beginnings on so many different levels that this time of life can be both exciting and nerve-racking at the exact same moment. This is true even if you aren't the one who made the decision to leave the old employ. Either finding a new job or looking for one that is far more fulfilling taps our reserves of courage, our sense of security, and, of course, our self-esteem. It's imperative, then, to find the positive in each and every job-searching situation and, most important, to keep every interview, rejection, and/or offer in as perfect a perspective as is manageable.

My client Josh first called me from his office on the West Coast to complain about what he felt was a lack of recognition and reward for all the effort he was "constantly contributing" to his job. Although he was considered part of a comprehensive team, his individual input (due to his own experience in this field) was critical to finding his financial institution new products to sell to their customers. He really was looking for some personal acknowledgment from his superiors, but, since I didn't fully understand (because—as we've all heard more than once—there is no *I* in team), I wanted him to get much clearer about what it was that he truly wanted from his job. I felt he wanted out but just couldn't let go because of the twenty years he had invested in that bank.

He needn't have worried quite so much because three weeks after our consultation, his bank was bought out and he, along with most of the senior staff, was let go. He was both angry and relieved at the same time, but with a wife and baby at home and another on the way, he needed to figure out his next steps before his bitty daughter took her first ones.

One of the initial things that I told Josh to do was to Find a New Job (or add HUGE opportunities to an existing one). Traditional dictates tell us that it's crucially important, while we're outside searching for both the right and the perfect job, that we leave our own outside lights on—on the front door entryway, on the front walkway, or, even better, on both. (If you have no outside lights, keep on the first light inside the front door.)

You should leave them on for at least three hours a day (preferably during the daytime, when they would not normally be on), illuminating, or actually "calling in," job opportunities. I actually have a red light outside my front door. My neighbors always know when some sort of big business is cooking around here because that light will stay on until the deal is signed, sealed, and, because that red light makes it much easier to find my house, delivered. Josh not only enacted this cure but did some of the others I am about to include herein, and inside of two weeks opportunity came knocking and he took a job as a freelance consultant to several local lending institutions. At last count he was making three times his previous salary. And the new baby was a bouncing and now well-supported boy.

Here are some more tips for creating luck as you Find a New Job:

• In Feng Shui, WATER is the element associated with how well everything in your job world is flowing. If things are coursing along exactly the way that you would like them to, then you should place some symbol of water directly inside the front door. Literally, a moving-water fountain will hasten the hallelujah when you come home with the perfect offer, but any symbol, such as a picture of the ocean or even of fish swimming inside a bowl, will also do the trick. Water is the element that represents career opportunities and advantages. Energetically, you can now influence a positive flow in the job search as well as bring in helpful contacts and, finally, job fulfillment. (If you are using an actual fountain, or any other physical water, be sure it's flowing INTO the house and not pointed out the front door, as that's where all your opportunities will go as well.)

Another client, Kara, a graphic designer looking to put her imprint in the workplace, put a full-fledged aquarium (eight goldfish and one black fish is the ticket) inside her front door when her own client list unexpectedly began to dry up. Within weeks of watching those little job seekers do *their* job, she called to tell me that she was doing a lot of traveling and was worried about taking on too much work and that while she was away her little fishies would perish. I told her to replace the aquarium with a picture of a meandering stream (less powerful than the actual water, but still potent enough) in her Career area and move the aquarium to her Wealth sector (back left-hand corner and entirely apropos). Soon her client count settled at exactly double where it was when she first called me, and she was easily able to afford a caring fish sitter and keep up with the workload!

- Hang metal wind chimes (with hollow rods or prongs) just outside the front door to help control movement within your career (and your life!). When hung with this particular intention, chimes will ring a breath of fresh air into your job search. If you don't have the wherewithal to hang chimes outside your front door because you share common space in an apartment hallway or for whatever reason, then get a small metal wind chime and hang it immediately inside your front door. If you are using the latter adjustment, then the ideal situation is to hang the chimes high in such a way that the clapper (the piece that hangs down and creates the movement) lightly touches the top of the front door when ever it opens.

- Locate the Career area inside your own home and bedroom (on our tic-tac-toe Bagua map that you overlay onto your floor plan, this is the bottom center area, usually where the front door actually is) and clear ALL clutter out of this area. Period. Really. End of sentence. ALL CLUTTER CLEARED! Next, clean your front door—especially if there is glass on it. This is the window to your future. Windex away! This is the place where opportunity will come knocking.

- Look at your front-door area very, very carefully. If the door sticks or cannot open all the way, then you are creating blockages in your job search and your life. Make sure

EVERYTHING around that doorway (doorbell, etc.) is in good working order and very soon so will you be.

- Use mirrors to open up lines of communication, expand lateral thinking, and create opportunity. The gold standard for using mirrors in the Career area is to install a pair of mirrors on opposite sides of your front entry at home. These should be affixed directly across from each other so that you must pass between them as you enter and exit. This is really efficacious when your front entry is narrow but still works no matter the architecture. You can use teeny-tiny mirrors (found at a crafts store), or you can embellish with elaborate and/or decoratively inspired larger ones. Every time you pass between them they will be working to expand, open up, and create new avenues of employment.

- The Elephant Cure. Place an elephant (wooden, ceramic—the material doesn't matter) on the floor by your front door and put a clear quartz crystal on his back. He will lend you his power, prudence, and sagacity and carry you through your job search like a king. (Feng Shui lore holds that the elephant is the bearer of the celebrated "wish granting" gem; in this case it's the clarity that you will now bring to procure the job of your dreams. Don't forget to take this elephant along on your job hunt. It guarantees a successful safari.

- Create a strong intention about what sort of job you want and then go claim it.

- While you are looking outside for employment, search inside for support by also inviting the universe along. One Universal affirmation that you can use comes from *The Game of Life and How to Play It,* by one of my favorite authors, Florence Scovel Shinn:

I have a perfect work
In a perfect way,
I give a perfect service
For perfect pay.

Empowering with each or any of these cures will dissolve potential obstacles along your way and will make your search clear, easy, and successful.

JOB INTERVIEW

I am positively sure that you will now have all the information necessary to pull off the most impressive job interview EVER! You cannot even imagine the calls I get from the previously out-of-work worrywart clients who now are nervous Nellies because of the slew of interviews coming through. And then the ones I get telling me gleefully all about how easily the interview went and how great the new job (the one they were immediately and on the spot offered) is going to be!

Take Jen, who had just graduated from college and was up for a position that she had dreamed about for four long years: a directorial assistant's job at a major television network. She had it all—the look, the attitude, along with the sweaty palms, the sleepless nights, and, of course, the pre–job interview jitters. She kept telling me that she just "had to" make a good first impression (critical!) and say all the right things, as well as be able to listen, react appropriately, and then remember everything the interviewer would be telling her.

I shared the interview Shui that never fails and then found out her interview didn't either. Last I heard she was working for one of Ted Turner's networks in Atlanta.

Here's some Lucky Day Shui to keep you occupied before, during, and directly after your interview(s).

PREINTERVIEW ENERGY ADVANTAGE

• Place a small brass bell in the center of the right-hand side of your desk. Or simply put the bell into the Children/ Creativity area of the main floor of your home (far, middle right-hand sector). Every time you prepare for an interview (or even send a résumé or cover letter or call HR to set up the first meet, for that matter), ring that bell. Preferably nine times. As the bell rings out loudly and clearly, so will your wishes and your intentions. You will also on a very subtle level be increasing your ability to be recognized for your own strengths and skills. They say that every time a bell rings, an angel gets its wings. I say, and you'll also get your job.

Okay, so with the communication conundrum covered, your thoughts are probably turning to what you should wear. There are three power-filled colors that anyone going on a job interview should integrate into their attire—either in a subtle or a big, bold way: navy blue and/or red, which can then be filtered with just a touch of white (we don't want you looking like a walking American flag, unless, of course, you're up for a stint on Capitol Hill). Red equals Fortune and Fame, or Recognition and Reward (in your area of expertise), and will fire up your opportunities to be recognized, to earn elder respect, and to receive all your just rewards. Deep, dark blue represents the color of Career. This supports your job search, your sense of self-esteem, and, bigger than anything, your life's journey. White is associated with tapping your Creativity and potential, so embracing this particular palette while enhancing these colorful energies will increase your personal power during any interview.

What might this look like? For women, you can simply include a dash of any of the three colors in your shoes, your scarf, or your bag. If a suit is indicated for your interview, make it navy or dark blue—this powerful color will immediately assert your competency as well as signal class *and* command respect— all at the same time. You can filter in the white in any number of ways—a white sweater, or a cami peeking through or even hidden as a piece of your lingerie. Some women have even been known to wear red lipstick to empower themselves through their successful mastectomies, so you can make this job-seeking operation your own success by adding a little red to the lips that will be doing all the talking and all the impressing as well. Red heels, well, I think that empowered visual about says it all.

Men have a much easier time incorporating blue into their interview ensemble, as this color is almost the de rigueur uniform for this one event. Again, a suit can be blue, as can the tie, or even the jeans if you are taking the more casual route. And guys, really, don't be afraid to bring on the heat and add a little red to fan the flames of recognition and respect. A smattering of red in your tie, a red belt, or even a burgundy briefcase will keep them burning to know more about you.

Personally, as a native New Yorker, I own almost nothing but black but will buy anything and everything red, white, and blue to somehow incorporate into my wardrobe on those days when I most need to make a great impression. My mantra is usually "THINK BIG," but in this specific case of dressing to impress, we can think small, subtle, and with the end result being that as you leave your interview, they will be thinking, "Sensational!"

NAIL IT!

Here are some more tips for nailing that interview:

- Try to always choose the seat farthest from the office door. If you can be looking at the door to the office where you've just entered, this will put you in the "command position." Very preferable and very *commanding*.

- Try not to sit under a heavy ceiling beam or any other heavy piece of decor hanging from the ceiling, like a chandelier. At a deep psychological level, this will make you feel "pressured" or "dwarfed" and might even cause you to feel claustrophobic.

- As you seat yourself, move your chair to either the right or the left, just the slightest bit. This gives you "ownership" over this space and puts you in the driver's seat.

- If you have any opportunity to choose a chair with a high back and arms, by ALL means, grab it. This not only lends you support but will bring balance to your negotiations.

- If you find that, while you are interviewing, your feet are facing the door, then gently and unassumingly shift so they are facing back into the room. I don't think I need to explain this one.

- Try as hard as possible to have some solid support in back of you. A solid wall, or even a window that has a tall building right outside of it, will do nicely.

- ALWAYS, and I mean always, send a thank-you note. I don't care how well or NOT well you think the interviewer thought of you, be gracious and grateful. Remember that each and every interview is an opportunity to hone your craft and your techniques. Add something that will remind them of you immediately. If you took the red heel advice, then a card with a pair of red stilettos on the front will move you to the front of their "thinking about you" pack (though that's probably not the best option for a more conservative employer). E-mails count only if you are incredibly good, and I mean Shakespearean good, at writing.

A Sniff of Courage

Need a quick whiff of courage before you head out to find the job of your dreams? Then try a few sniffs of this Lucky little blend before you go, and before you know it, you'll be smelling the sweet scent of interview success.

Courage Blend
All oils are 100% essential oils.

9 drops of ylang-ylang
4 drops bergamot
2 drops melissa
9 drops sandalwood

Blend these oils with ½ cup of any "carrier" oil (like olive, peanut, or my personal favorite, grapeseed, which you can get at any health-food store), and then take a big breath of this blend into the nose right before you embark on the interview. You can even make this mobile by carrying Courage on a hankie or cotton ball in a little Ziploc bag that you can open every time you need an extra shot. Speaking of having a shot, as with any essential oils, NEVER, EVER drink them.

FIRST DAY ON THE NEW JOB

Everyone all around you is busy and knows their way through the back alleys of the office, and you feel like a fish out of water. Don't! Soon enough, there will be newbies coming to you for sage advice. All you need to do is activate the energies and let the Universe handle the rest. Here's what to do.

Whether big office or small cubicle or the newer work space, the "officle," you'll want to add a touch of "you" to the space so that your fins start to swim in sync with all your other office mates—you may even get a leg up on some of the more ambitious shark types.

Place a picture or two of someone in your industry whom you admire in the back center of the new space. This will give you constant and consistent inspiration and a buddy to talk to when there may be some shy types around, tending to leave you a bit lonely while you're still the new kid on the block.

In the same space—back, middle, or center—place a symbol that reminds you of your desired rewards or goals. Any symbol placed here will support your intentions to be recognized and rewarded in your wonderful new position.

And, last, take the brass bell from home (the one that helped get you the job in the first place!), and put it in the center of the right-hand side of your desk at work. Let it continue to ring out your reputation whether you pick it up and swing it or not.

The pictures, the symbols of your goals, and even the bell will give anyone who wants to give you a chance reason enough to start a conversation. Before long, it'll all be flowing, as will office mates into your cubicle for all your sage advice.

STALE OR STALLED BUT STAYING

Let's face it, even the best job in the world can sometimes get a little stale or a bit stalled and make you start to second-guess why you're waking up and getting glam every day to do the same old, same old. Even my wand starts to wind down after a while!

Shelly, one of my favorite clients in the entire Universe, called me one day to banter about her belief that it might be time for her to move on from a job that she had dreamed about FOR-EVER. She was bored. Shelly felt like she was in a radio rut (she's a producer of a nationally syndicated talk-radio show). Even though she was totally devoted and dedicated to "her team," she was beginning to cave under the day-to-day pressures. There were just too many tasks that required her to push the glamour of booking the famous guest aside for more than a minute in favor of getting the rest of the job done—and those moments were starting to take a toll.

She needed emergen-Chi, a quick boost of energy, a fresh dose of enthusiasm, and mighty motivation, and she needed it right then and there because she really is one of the best in her jobs, stale, stalled, or energetically at the ready.

This is what I told her to do:

- Look around your entire house (and office, if applicable) for little "leaks" and not so obvious "outages." Leaky faucets or, conversely, clogged drains are problems in the arteries of our homes (and offices) and are reflected in our outer experiences. Lightbulbs that have blown need to be replaced. Pronto. This act alone can bring some brightness back to the blah job. We really do call Feng Shui "acupuncture for the home (and office)" because our living environments mirror back to us what goes on not only inside us but all around us as well. For this reason alone, when we understand that what happens around us can, on a very subtle but very strong level, influence every other area of our lives, then it makes perfect sense to address dripping faucets and flickering lights. Once you do this inventory, you will have taken charge of creating a more functioning environment, and everything that you thought was broken, boring, stale, or stalled can take on a whole shiny new patina.

Just ask Shelly! Although she did her due diligence and fixed all the faucets at home, and after she had located the cleaning crew at work to assess and address her office issues, she finally realized that what she needed was simply a vacation—she didn't want to leave her job after all. I, of course, still sitting and writing about fortune and luck at my own computer, got a postcard from Hawaii not too long after that. Aloha, Shelly, and have a mai tai on me!

SIGNING A CONTRACT
(OR THE ART IN THE DEAL)

If you are in the advantageous position of signing a contract or executing a deal, there is one especially fast, especially effective, and entirely prosperity-laden cure that will attract great success to the transaction. And, go figure, it's called The Prosperity Signature! Seriously, if you take a look at some of the most famous John Hancocks (including his) in the world, you will see that exactly what I am about to tell you must really work, because from Ben Franklin to Donald Trump (along with a host of the wise and wealthy in between), this special way of signature signing is evidently routine for the fortunate and the fabulous.

Quick Tips to Keep Your
Career Captivating

- Take care of your files! You know by now the calamity that clutter causes in our lives and in our jobs, so make sure you have a handle on your files or a cabinet around them. And NEVER, EVER put files on the floor, especially to the left of you. According to this tradition, this infraction will push you right out the office door and onto the unemployment line.
- Put a small convex mirror on the top of the screen of your computer. This will not only enhance a sense of security if your back faces the opening of your office space but also attract energy to your space, as that's just what these mirrors are supposed to do.
- Speaking of computers, your screensaver should reflect something either motivational and/or inspirational to and for you. If it's moving, all the better as this will create a constant flow in the land of your Chi, which is reflected in your job.
- If possible, bring fresh flowers to your work space to bring fresh Chi to same. They should be placed on the top center of your desk if possible. If there just isn't enough space there for a vase full of fresh cuts, even a little stalk of bamboo sticking up on the upper left-hand side of your desk will bring on the fortune, bring on the luck, and liven things up. Always try to use uneven numbers, unless otherwise instructed, when you're making bamboo work for you.
- Mountain means support. Put a small picture of a mountain on the back of your desk chair (with the mountain facing your back), and you will soon find yourself scaling new professional heights.

Activate Your Publishing Career

This secret can be used by anyone who works in magazine, book, or Web-related publishing. The key to this cure is that it rises and sets with the sun. Literally, I mean it, a symbol of the sun can make your reputation rise sky-high in the world of the written word.

One of my own editors called me one day and inquired whether there was anything she could do to further her own career inside the magazine she was (and still is!) working for. (It's funny how some people really "get" how this stuff works and have a million different applications once they open to it.) She wanted to know if there happened to be any specific "Publishing Shui." So, for those of you in this highly esteemed field:

Find any image of the sun (a photo, a mirror with sun rays around the edge, a copper sun that you see at landscaping stores) and place it in the center or middle of the back wall of your office. Bigger is not necessarily better in Feng Shui, so if you share an office or have a really small space, you can still make it sunny back there—just use a little sun.

My client Ricky was really serious about this. She went to the NASA website and downloaded a photo of the sun (talk about going straight to the source!). The photo just happened to have been taken on my last birthday, to boot! Big forces "at work" here. EXACTLY one week after she hung the sun, she found out the moon and the stars were about to be all hers, too. Two of her immediate supervisors had both left their jobs on the same day, and even though Ricky had just been promoted from fact checker to assistant editor only a few short months earlier, she was considered for and confirmed in one of those upward and onward advisory positions.

(You'll have to wait to read the Fame section to see what happened to one of those senior editors who left that same magazine and who used this same cure. Believe me, it's worth the wait and worth the read and, if you are in the business of publishing, worth basking in these rays to help you secure your space under the sun and shine, baby, shine!)

As for me, well, sometimes even as I sit inside my own office, I still have to put on shades.

Ancient custom holds that how you hold the pen doesn't really matter, but how you sign on the bottom line can and WILL substantially add to your own. Begin the first letter of your first name with a firm, upward stroke and end the last letter of your last name in the same exact way. This can be done even if, like mine, the letters in your name don't really lend themselves to this success-full signature. (It's a bit hard for me to make the *E* in Ellen end upward, and the same is true for the *t* in Whitehurst.) But you'd better believe that when the deal is on the table and waiting for me to sign, I never forget to remember onward and UPWARD—right before I leave with new contracts in hand and immediately before I head to the bank.

Firm first letter up and firm last letter the same way. Firm deal done!

Now, congratulations!

	2	
Wealth and Prosperity	Fame and Reputation	Relationship, Romance, and Marriage
Family, Friends, and Ancestors	Health	Children and Creativity
Knowledge and Self-Cultivation	Career	Helpful People and Travel

WHENEVER I TRY to explain the energies associated within our environments, I also try to show that "There are more things in Heaven and Earth, Horatio," as Shakespeare quite adeptly put it, "than are dreamt of in your philosophy." This includes you and me. Yes, indeed, this arena is about book learning and getting better grades, but it is also about acquiring wisdom and, hardest of all, learning to love yourself so that others may love you just as much, if not more!

As we keep encountering, life is about growth, and this yearning, this desire or compulsion to grow, stems from our inherent wish to know more about the world around us, the world about us, but, especially, the world inside us—the one that guides us with inner reserves of wisdom, intuitive abilities, our interests, our internal compass, and anything that helps us to assimilate new ideas and activities into our lives. It is these exercises of the mind that make us better people, able to appreciate ourselves a little bit, or even a whole lot, more. The more we learn about ourselves— our likes, our dislikes, what makes us tick, and what helps us tock—will also open all the doors necessary for us to push our limits and take off to wiser parts unknown, until, of course, they become known and no longer unwise or unfamiliar.

Familiar is a good word to use here because this whole arena is about just the opposite. It's about learning new things to add to the wonderfully wise beings that we already are. But then we find out our options are limitless, as are our opportunities. We can use this space to allow ourselves new opportunities to grow—in insight, in awareness, and, more often than not, in fortune and luck. The adjustments associated with this sector will inspire, heal, and encourage you. They will cause excellence for you, for your life, and for your worth. And you are worth it. It is my hope and my prayer that with our last breath we will ALL, every one of us, still be learning something new. Because that means ALL of us, every one of us, will still be loving our own individual selves enough, and then that ripple effect will, with the help of our wisdom, heal this planet.

Knowledge and Self-Cultivation is located in the front, or lower, left-hand corner of your home, bedroom, or office, or whatever space you wish to energize. The best choice of color here is a midnight or deep, dark blue and the associative element is earth. The number to use here is 8. Therefore, a pretty standard way to activate this section is to keep eight blue stones (along with some informative magazines or classic books or any symbol of something you're yearning to learn about).

TICK, TOCK . . . THIS CLOCK'S FOR YOU

Every time I speak in public and I am explaining the energies represented on the Bagua map that we use, I always have to take time to make sure that all the people in the audience, especially the women, understand that this energy called Knowledge and Self-Cultivation is exactly that— a place focused on learning more and cultivating what you learn so that it becomes second nature to you. When I get to this particular space clients often and immediately think I'm talking about how to improve their kids' grades (which this energy addresses as well), or, if my client is switching careers and has to study to get some additional expertise, like getting a broker's license (which this energy addresses, too), that he or she can "adjust" or "cure" this arena and then that will be that.

Most people seem to find it difficult to see the expansive nature of this arena, that is, of course, until I patiently and explicitly explain to them that this space is precisely about learning to love themselves and give to themselves BEFORE they give to the whole rest of the world. It's about learning to do what you love and see how much better (in record time) your whole life gets. And then this "butterfly effect" will give everyone around you their wings as well. To me, this is the essence of Wisdom.

I have learned so many things in my years of listening to client concerns, and one of them is that self-sacrifice and martyrdom run rampant in ladyland. (To be honest, I also grew up in a household where my mother never—I mean NEVER— thought of herself first.) I see this habitual *art* of self-sacrifice constantly. The kids, the job, the husband, the neighbors—everyone else comes first on the agenda BEFORE you. But what kind of self-honoring is there in that? What are you teaching your children? That everyone else matters more than you do? I agree that there always has to be the one well that everyone can come and feel safe dipping their cup into, but if you never refill the well, well, where's the sense in that? Empty is empty is empty. Activating the energies of this *gua* equals refill.

When I see a woman who puts everyone and everything else ahead of her own needs, I see a woman who will eventually empty her own well good and dry, and then, when the next person comes with their ladle and tries to dig what they perceive to be their share of Her, they'll hear the scratch, scratch, scratch of that ladle hitting against that empty well. This, then, can promote illness, injury, conflict, and, someday, disease for the person who hasn't taken the time or energy to stop and refuel herself.

We are always in a hurry. We make ourselves and everyone around us so many promises. We'll always read that new book tomorrow, start working out next week, try that new restaurant when the kids don't have baseball or lacrosse or are learning how to make a Mentos jump six feet in the air after dropping it into a cola bottle for their school science fair. With the advent of technology, life in general has sped up, and we just can't seem to find the time to slow down long enough to nurture or nourish our own selves and our own souls.

Knowledge and Self-Cultivation should be about something you always wanted to do but never found the time to pursue. Piano lessons. Line dancing. Painting. Find out what you love to do. And then do that. And then do it regularly, once a month, if possible. Now look at the message you're putting out there: "I'm worth it." And this time you will truly believe it.

Perhaps better even than this knowledge of your self-worth is that once you begin to prove this truth to yourself and everyone else around you, the Universe will provide all the time for you to pursue your passion. As an added bonus, you'll also be amazed at how easily every other little thing appears to get taken care of as well. Instead of begrudging the battle to beat the traffic after staying at work just five minutes longer than everyone else, you'll feel beautifully full, right before you take on the world.

So find something you love to do (a hobby . . . I know, I know . . . but just go with me here) and then, like the ads say, "Just do it." When you take care of you, you will then become a better person for it and so will everyone who comes in contact with you. You will be the beacon, teaching all those around you that being "self-ish" means giving back to your self, your soul, your sense of self-love, so that you can give your all to everyone else. LOVE YOU FIRST. The rest will follow. Only then will you fall in love all over again and so will everyone else in your life—with you. Immediately! And, I promise, instead of constantly feeling like you've been hit by a train, you will feel like you are always walking on air as you glide to the next station for your special day at the museum in the city.

P.S. Manicures, pedicures, massage, and working out are all considered "maintenance" in my book. Find a hobby. Those ain't that. But here are some important tips to start now:

- Take a calendar of some sort (day planner, Palm Pilot, or cell phone) and pick one day a month to nourish and nurture yourself doing something you love. One afternoon, even. Three hours. You can manage three hours. This should be something you do completely by YOURSELF (lunch with the ladies doesn't count). You need to make an appointment with yourself and then keep to it like you need a root canal. If you had that kind of pain, you'd never miss that dental appointment, right? Same thing here. Make an appointment and then don't break it no matter what. Try to schedule six months out, and you won't believe all the great stuff that will begin to happen in your life inside of six days.

- Find the lower left-hand area of your home or bedroom (Knowledge and Self-Cultivation) and put a comfy chair there with a comfy throw and some comfy pillows. Put your feet up and read a good book. The energy of books is most at home here, especially if they are about something you want to learn.

- Hang a bell in this area with the intent of bringing clarity, ideas, ideals, and movement to your intentions. If you simply cannot find the time to honor yourself by picking up a hobby and sticking to this commitment, the bell will help create that space while ringing in new projects and plans. Ring in the refill when the gauge is running on empty.

BIRTHDAY SHUI:
GIVE THE GIFT THAT KEEPS ON GIVING

Lauren called to share that she was planning her mother's sixty-fifth birthday—a monumental challenge since her mother was impossible to please when it came to this specific special day. For years, no matter the thought, money, or time spent behind any

gift or party, her mother, whom Lauren and her siblings nick-
named "the Beehive" (get the stinging picture?), was simply
never satisfied.

But for the Beehive's sixty-fifth birthday, Lauren was determined to impress her mother with an unforgettably wonderful
day, so she came to me for some honey and some help.

I suggested Lauren follow the ever successful Birthday Shui
ritual, which she did (see below). She called me the day after
their big shindig and told me she had never seen her mother so
happy in her life. "My mother thought it was the most beautiful
birthday, and, brace yourself, she actually softened up and cried!"
Lauren recounted the fact that the family had put so much
thought into this one event, it impressed her mother to tears. I
found myself choking back a little sniffle myself. God, I just love
this stuff!

Needless to say, birthdays—either experiencing one for yourself or planning a celebration for another—are charged with lots
of expectations, both spoken and unspoken. By using one special
Feng Shui cure, the birthday of anyone's dreams is guaranteed to
deliver their dearest desires!

The Feng Shui age old birthday ritual:

- Buy five helium-filled balloons. Make sure there is one balloon of each of the following colors: red, yellow, white, pink,
  and purple (NEVER use balloons that are blue or green or
  black!).

- Tie a tail on each balloon with nine or eighteen inches of
  red (there's that auspicious color again) ribbon, string, thread,
  or yarn.

- Include a black felt-tip marker with this gift and the following instructions:

- With the black pen, have the birthday celebrant write one wish on each balloon that best describes his or her heart's desires.

- When the celebrant is finished writing each wish, on a clear and sunny day, from an open space (like a park or backyard), gently release one of the "wish" balloons at a time.

- When the balloons have all vanished from sight, then the wishes have entered the stream from which all life flows.

- It is promised that sometime before the next birthday either one or possibly ALL of those wishes will have come true.

Now, why waste time at the mall when you can blow up your dreams and then release any thought that they won't come true. There's a HAPPY birthday.

GRADUATION DAY

My clients Bob and Beth had hosted the wedding of their only daughter the summer before in their own backyard and were now gearing up for another emotional rite of passage: the college graduation of their only son, Paul. Beth wanted badly to make this a magical celebration for Paul not only because he was graduating from a prestigious university with honors (that he held for the entire four years), but also because he helped put himself through school with a scholarship while also holding down TWO (!!) part-time positions. And part of Paul's motivation to take on such financial responsibility was so that Beth and Bob could help put a canopy over their beloved daughter's head and some exotic and delicious canapés on a beautiful buffet table at her wedding some twelve months earlier. Paul, clearly an exceptional kid, deserved an extraordinary event.

Whether the person you love is graduating from pre-K, walking across a stage with a doctorate in hand, or heading toward her first year as a medical intern, the word *graduation* can conjure a host of feelings and flights of fancy. Moving across or onto the next stage, graduation marks the ending of one and the beginning of another, and there are always questions about what waits around the corner. Are there any opportunities or too many new realities to handle at once? Or, heaven forbid, are some disasters or dangers lurking?

Beth and Bob wanted to bring future big fortune and luck to Paul's graduation get-together. We've all faced these stages at one point or another, like Sean, who wanted to see his son Mark finally forget the clam digging on Cape Cod and get his GED so he could eventually look for work on Wall Street, where he then could use his inherently savvy money and math skills. To every person who wants to send their graduate out into the world with an energetic edge, here's the way to give 'em wings and let them soar;

RITUALS AND GIFTS FOR THE LUCKY GRADUATE:

- It's long been acknowledged that if you want to bring your angels and guides out of campus housing and along for the next ride of your life, then you should find some statue on campus and, at a time immediately prior to graduating, rub the nose (or some other part) of same statue for luck and fortune to help make your dreams a reality. This will help bring along both their and your luck to commencement, to infinity, and beyond.

• Under the cap and gown, the graduate should wear certain colors to attain certain energetic advantages. Wearing anything white signifies respect for all the arts, while gold recognizes the tremendous value and worth of the sciences. Brown represents stability and grounding, both virtues and qualities that most graduates can use in spades. Any and/or all combinations of these colors represent panoramic academic achievements. There's also a graduation fashion-nation that says those commencing should don flat shoes to symbolize their steady stepping into their new lifestyle. But from a girl who thinks Birkenstock should make a stiletto, well . . . just consider me as delivering the message, not the farewell address (because if I were, I'd be wearing tall Jimmy Choos to the podium!).

• Speaking of the cap, traditionally these mortarboards have a small pocket inside to hold an extra bit of fortune and luck—as in a charm of some sort. I always gift graduates three faux Chinese coins tied together on a piece of red ribbon, string, thread, or yarn (a very traditional way to garner great and good fortune and luck for ANYONE, especially the trembling graduate). Any good-luck symbol tucked tightly inside the cap will add health, happiness, and prosperity to the graduation ceremony. Just make sure the graduate NEVER tips the cap back—that's a strict no-no in the world of customs and traditions and is thought to bring bad luck. If the tradition at your school dictates that you throw your cap into the air upon commencement, you can either put your name (in dry-erase marker so sweating won't cause it to run) inside your hat and go look for it after the ceremony ends, or just go ahead and throw caution to the wind and know that your luck will return to you threefold from this flying trifold.

• Waking Up to Your New Life, or the Red Cloth Cure:
Graduation clearly and considerably involves someone moving from within one society to join another and also clearly
and considerably can cause some jangly nerves and create
questions about what's next and who's next and how and
when that's all going to happen. The Red Cloth Cure will
smooth this transition and enhance life in any number of
ways, but the power of individual intention cannot be under-
scored enough here. Does the graduate need to bring some
vitality to his or her efforts or get a healthy attitude about the
future? Does she need a boost of spirits and energies as she
sets out to fulfill her next dramas and next BIG dreams? In
order for all graduates to get a degree of clarity regarding
their future, they need to get a red cloth or a red sheet as big
as the space between the mattress and the box spring of their
bed. This cloth should go in that space. And then every night
before these aspiring achievers go to sleep, they should get
really clear about what they think the next leg of their journey looks like to and for them. Focus, sleep, and then
achieve—that's the mantra associated with this time-tested
adjustment that really does leave you "to sleep, perchance to
dream" right before you make those postgraduate dreams
come true!

• Place a globe of the world in the graduate's room in the
Fame arena (back center or middle of the room) and light it
somehow. Some globes already come lit from within (as do
some graduates), while others need a little more help . . . the
globe, that is. Just grab a small spotlight from any home-
improvement store and shine it at the globe. This will bring
opportunities to graduates from every corner of the . . . you
guessed it . . . globe. Even if they start right in their own

The Graduate and the Golden Ring . . . A Perfect Gift

If Benjamin had paid more heed to Mrs. Robinson's wedding ring, then maybe, just maybe, he and her daughter could have met, easily married, and made that mint in plastics just like the neighbor told him to do at his own graduation pool party. Okay, for anyone who hasn't seen *The Graduate*, this is a dated (but really worth the rental) reference, and, also, a segue.

Gold rings make a really great graduation gift. In fact, it's so great a tradition that West Point established the first class ring in the early 1800s. Clearly the idea took off and has stuck around and there's a reason why. The custom of wearing rings and pins dates back to the ancient Egyptians, who believed that the seals and signets on the rings would ward off evil, bad luck, and even death. They also knew that wearing these symbols would bode well for victory over many different circumstances. Hence it's the perfect gift for the perfect graduate.

A gold ring, in particular, represents nobility and is recognized to represent wealth, prosperity, and success. Just in case, the ring should be worn on the third finger of the right hand to hearken and help all the strength, courage, health, and abundance that will now come full circle.

backyard (as Paul's did when a friend of his dad found out that Paul was an art history major in college. Bob's friend had just invested in a new gallery opening in a nearby city and a new "art-nership" was born!).

3		
Wealth and Prosperity	Fame and Reputation	Relationship, Romance, and Marriage
Family, Friends, and Ancestors	Health	Children and Creativity
Knowledge and Self-Cultivation	Career	Helpful People and Travel

THE ENERGIES ATTRACTED to this sector of the Feng Shui navigational map are all about, well, family, friends, and ancestors. Go figure. It's about what you inherit from your family of origin. That means anything from your blue eyes to the blue delft bowl that Great-aunt Rose left especially for you as a reminder of your bond. It's about your lineage, your line, your family tree, and even the saplings that you'd really love to belong to you as well. We all know a family that we wish we were a part of, even if just for the great Bar Mitzvah parties that they throw for their own coming-of-age sons.

This area is all about family dynamics and friendly fire. It is the place that should support you and bring you confidence in your abilities and your talents or should at least bring you good friends who will do the same. It's about you reaching your full potential and branching out and doing your thing and never having to hear one word of criticism about any of your choices.

We all know that nothing's that easy where family and friends are concerned, which is exactly why it's so important that we understand specifically where this area is (middle of the left-hand portion of the main floor, office, bedroom, or any other space you spend a lot of time in) and why tweaking or activating it can become a lifeline. Because the influence these energies have over so many other areas of your life (think "Mother" and, well, enough said) are so vast and can affect so many decisions you make, I cannot stress enough the importance of proactively tending and weeding this personal garden, the one that grows your roots.

This section will talk about setting elemental enhancements and the how/what/where/why they can help in every conceivable arena of your life as well as underscoring the obvious importance of what is called in Feng Shui "Descendant's LUCK," or not only the energies that have come before you (and that carry on through your DNA) but also what opportunities can be created and line your personal path with roses, which you will now be able to stop and smell, maybe with some terrific friends along for the stroll. Support, foundations, growth, relationships, self-expression, and reaching fullest potential can all be summed up in three little words: Family, Friends, and Ancestors. And it makes perfect sense that the element associated with these energies is wood and the color is the healthy green of growth. The number of this arena is 3, so three wooden frames with pictures of friends or family members planted particularly in this space will always help you feel your rightful space on this planet.

THANKSGIVING DAY SHUI

Thanksgiving is the ultimate day of gratitude and thanks, right? Yet we all know that holidays that bring families together are often both looked forward to and dreaded all at the same time. This crazy combo of feelings can be caused by just how much we all invest in wanting these special days to unfold in a smooth, stress-free, and enjoyable way—especially Thanksgiving. With its emphasis on both appetizers and appreciation, this holiday is usually stuffed full with both. Just ask Deb!

Married for more than twenty years, Deb had never hosted the family Thanksgiving before and was bound and determined to make everything absolutely perfect—from menu to table decor to even, no kidding, making sure that the furniture around her house made her guests feel comfy and at ease. Yes, Deb wanted it all. She was most concerned about her older sister, a critical chick with a gourmet palate and a forked tongue who had a particular gift for getting under Deb's skin.

One shade shy of frantic, Deb called me and asked if there was anything from the world of ancient tradition and custom to help make this modern celebration one that could WOW! Of *course* there is. Here's the menu that I offered up:

- Use yellow mums as your choice of floral decoration and be sure to have them placed strategically throughout the house. These plants, along with fresh-cut florals, are known to usher in both tranquillity and peace while also bringing a handy dash of recognition for your efforts. If you are visiting (LUCKY YOU!), bring a fresh yellow mum to the host and/or hostess. You will be creating a heaping helping of harmony and happiness for your hosts, which will then, in true Karmic fashion, come back to you three times over. Now, there's something to be thankful for!

- Use side lighting (table lamps) instead of overhead lighting. Harsh or over-the-head lights can create shadows, which in turn, on a very subtle level, can cause depressing energies to be invited for dinner as well. Overhead lighting is also thought to lead to creating anxiety in the atmosphere—something we try to avoid at all costs at any family gathering!

- Cover your table with a cloth cover (thought to absorb any negative vibrations or floating discord). For this occasion, paper just won't cut it!

- Place a flat mirror (any size) under the centerpiece of the table to ground the energy of the room and reflect back the wish for health and harmony.

• Serve almond rice cookies (along with whatever age-old pumpkin pie tradition your family enjoys) at the end of this feast. This Feng Shui "secret" not only brings sweetness to the day's events but also adds an extra dollop of fortune and luck (according to the ancients) to the table and those who sit around it. (Note: If you are not the host but a guest wishing for a smooth, peace-filled, and enjoyable holiday, then bring the cookies. And then I'll bet you'll get the best part of the bird, too!)

• Last, try to fold in, either to the stuffing or to the stuffed, some combination of apples, grapes, corn, and pomegranates. Since I learned about this bit of Turkey Day luck, I like to now simply tie these ingredients inside little gift bags and give them as a party favor—they are guaranteed to bring peace and prosperity!

Acorn Lore

There is a story told in many traditions regarding the lovely acorn that falls from the mighty oak tree. It says that there is an enchanted forest with a race of acorn people who all live in an ageless oak tree that stands higher than the heavens in the center of this forest. Every one of these people from the age of five to sixty-five wears a bracelet that has one word inscribed on it... NOW. Those who are younger than five and older than sixty-five don't need to wear this adornment as they instinctively understand the gift that being in the present moment brings. Each acorn person has a special gift that is recognized and nurtured and that they share with their loving community. They all love one another without condition and they all allow themselves to be loved (receive love!) while never judging or condemning any other.

They say that these acorn people have scattered their acorns to the wind in the hopes that when anyone finds an acorn that person will come to embrace their own special gifts and talents (that only they were born with) as well as committing themselves to sharing that gift. From this they will then receive the ultimate gift . . . DIVINE, NEVER ENDING LOVE!

Acorn Squash Soup

The acorn squash got its name because of its similarity in shape and symbol to the acorn.

1 tablespoon vegetable oil
1 red onion, finely chopped
1 small acorn squash, seeded and cubed
1 cup chicken broth
1 cup vegetable broth
1/4 cup plain yogurt
1/4 cup cream
Pinch of salt and pinch of cayenne pepper
1/4 cup sour cream (for garnish)
Pinch of ginger (the magical ingredient) and pinch of nutmeg (for garnish)

1. Heat the oil in a saucepan over medium heat. Add the chopped onion and sauté until it has turned translucent and just begins to brown. Add the acorn squash and the broth. Lower the heat and let simmer until all

the vegetables are tender, about a half hour. Let this mixture cool.

2. Into a blender, add the vegetable mixture and the yogurt and blend into a puree. Return this mixture to the saucepan and stir in the cream until it is the desired consistency. Add the salt and pepper to taste and cook over low heat until heated through (about eight minutes).

3. Transfer the soup to previously warmed bowls and top each with a spoonful of sour cream and a sprinkle of the ginger and the nutmeg.

Go outside and gather some acorns and decorate the tabletop with these loving "little people" while you enjoy this transformative soup to nourish and nurture you in both the here and the NOW! And don't forget to be so grateful for this very GOOD and thanks-filled day.

MOTHER'S DAY

Sheila called me last year on Mother's Day weekend to once again complain about how she had to spend the holiday at her mother-in-law's house instead of with her own mom. Now, logistically this makes sense, since her husband's mom lives about fourteen minutes from their house and her mother lives about fourteen hundred miles away. But that's really not even the part that always amazes me about this yearly complaint. It's that Sheila really loves her mother-in-law and always treats her more like a mom than she does her own mother. I'm not judging here,

I'm only observing that Mother's Day, as an event or a celebration, can be fraught with emotions, good, bad, or just plain not even close to reality.

The reason Sheila has such a wonderful rapport with her "friend" and mom-in-law, Jeanne, is that Jeanne treats Sheila like the daughter she never had, AND like an adult, while Sheila's own mom treats her like she's still twelve.

"I swear," Sheila tells me, "my mother actually said to me the other day when I was talking about all my friends doing the Zone Diet, 'Well, if all your friends jumped off a cliff—!' "

You get the rest. *Wear clean underwear in case you get hit by a bus. Don't make that face or it'll freeze like that. Who really wrote that history essay for you?* Oooops, that last part might just be a piece of my past. But you get it. Sheila has one "mom" who values her for the adult daughter-in-law she is, and another who still tells her to be careful not to poke her eye out with her #2 pencil. She calls this a problem? I call it pretty LUCKY with a teensy dab of daughter guilt on top.

I suggested that this year she might want to do something special for both of these wonderful women that would show her appreciation for their totally different relationships but nurture them BOTH nonetheless. "Let's look at Mother's Day as an opportunity to honor ALL the maternal energies that help to shape our lives and try to give back just a smidge of what we've received." She agreed that this year, instead of bemoaning the fact that she was spending time with one and not with the other, she would honor them both, but wanted to know just exactly how to do that. I gave her my professional suggestions (see below!) and she called days later, completely thrilled with their day, with the positive results, and with the opportunity to look at this annual enigma from another perspective.

I have more than my share of clients who have more than their share of issues with their mothers. There are sonnets written, songs sung, and years upon years of emotional baggage sometimes weighing us down as a result of this one cord that binds. Umbilical or not, that attachment is real, and often it has long-lasting and tremendous impact on our lives.

One of the reasons that Mother's Day was even established was because late in the 1600s, in jolly old England, most of the servants lived with their employers. For one Sunday a year, these mums were encouraged to return home to their families (which, if you were my mother, even that one Sunday would still involve a tremendous amount of servitude. But my mother was really smart, and my guess is she probably would have chosen to stay at the manor and read a good book instead. But I digress). So, in England, as in early Greece way before that, there became a day that Mom could spend with the family, preferably being adored and not working. They called it Mothering Sunday. This has evolved into our present-day celebrations.

The Chinese, however, don't even have one specific day to honor Mom, but rather believe that she is the ultimate symbol and quintessence of family harmony and almost solely responsible for keeping the peace and keeping everyone together. Whew. They hold that she should be honored every day. Now, see, I buy that! For some of us, well, Mother Knows Best. She's the comfort and the kindness, the wisdom and the well, whether we actually popped from her womb or not. For others the word itself conjures thirty years of therapy that still hasn't made a dent. But, and there's no denying it, for all of us, MOTHER means something, and there's a Sunday in May when we can express whatever that something is.

According to Feng Shui, there is an actual location inside our homes that honors the mother, and it is in the back right-hand corner of the main floor, or could also be considered in that same space of your bedroom. If, like Sheila, you feel distance (on ANY level) between you and your mom, you could, as tradition suggests, put a light on in this area to enlighten or even lighten up the relationship that the two of you share while at the same time creating a charge between you. Having her picture here helps enliven this enhancement. Giving your mom a lamp or candles, and also instructing her where to put them, is a great way to create this connection between you.

For those who really want to take the reins and energize the Mother area, it is advised to place a picture of a mare in that far back right-hand corner of the bedroom. This image of the female horse symbolizes the essence of motherhood, while also helping Mom to safeguard the resilience of the family. This little adjustment helped heal a rift between my client Joe and his mother when he quietly put a small statue of a horse in the Mother sector of his bedroom. He recounted that after a few weeks of them not speaking to each other (over something he couldn't even remember!) she called him one day out of the blue and they talked about hurts and healing and his childhood for hours. It was both the statue and his intention that brought the healing, and his action and then his expectant attitude that caused this loving change. Other clients of mine who have had abusive relationships with their moms can still sometimes be convinced to place a picture or statue of a mare here just so they can begin their own healing process—equinely, um, I mean, equally important when they are carrying loads of pain and resentment.

There is even some age-old and sage advice for moms with unruly kids or moms who may have an ongoing conflict with any of her offspring. This is how it goes:

- Take a picture of the child and one of the mom (see, anyone can do this) and face them toward each other, placing mother and child face-to-face, so to speak.

- Then wrap the two photos together ninety-nine times with red ribbon, string, thread, or yarn (again with the cords that bind!).

- Now take this little red picture package and throw it into any body of moving water (long renowned as representing the womb of the Universal mother). Remember, no matter where you live, you can access this moving body of water in any stream, river, pond, or lake!

By doing this you shall enact a resolution to the dilemmas and/or issues within a twenty-seven-day period (this is a standard amount of time accorded to many Feng Shui rituals). Remember, this is according to ancient customs, but I have clients who have used this cure with great success and find that this water ritual has really saved their family a whole bunch of tears.

THE BEST GIFTS FOR MOM

- Bamboo is a great gift that is thought to energize, bring solid support, and add longevity to every area of her life. There are even numbers of stalks of bamboo that you can give her to show support in specific areas of her life. If she is looking for or at a career change, give her one stalk of bamboo. Two if she's looking for a partner, five if her health is of any concern, seven if her kids are, or eight if she's looking for a little spare cash.

Mother's Day Milk Bath

Although milk may be pasteurized in our modern age, it still retains mystical qualities and magical uses in addition to serving as a practical and staple source of nourishment. Milk is considered a gift from the gods, one that enhances your own abilities to give and receive love. That result can occur whether you are bathing in it or adding to it chocolate syrup and a spritz of seltzer and drinking it. This particular bath recipe will soothe, calm, restore, and renourish Mom in both body and spirit. Adding fresh mint and parsley to the bath adds personal empowerment to Mom's life. The milk will give her a fresh and softened perspective on her daily routine. The honey adds sweetness and the salt detoxifies. All in all, draw your mother this bath on Mother's Day and you will draw some mighty powerful and mighty good energies her way. She deserves it.

> *1/2 cup golden honey (any honey will do)*
> *1/2 cup whole milk*
> *1/2 cup either Epsom salts or sea salt*
> *3 crushed fresh mint leaves*
> *A few sprigs of fresh parsley*

Mix the first two ingredients in a bowl and add the crushed mint leaves and the parsley. Run the bathwater and pour in the 1/2 cup of Epsom salts and let dissolve. Right before Mom gets in the bath, add the honey and milk mixture from the bowl and, for goodness sake, LET HER SOAK for at least twenty minutes.

- Any statue of an elephant gifts her with luck and fortune, but a white one will bring her her heart's desire within a short space of time. Sightings of a white elephant are considered mystical in many traditions (like the white buffalo in mythical Native American lore). If Mom isn't big on the whole elephant thing, white hens and white rabbits (go ask Alice), as well as horses and butterflies, are also considered to bring on the magic!

- Any jewelry made of jade is considered to gift her with the qualities of healing, health, and longevity. Jade is supposed to carry miraculous powers. Long live the mom who wears or carries jade.

- A real live rosemary plant symbolizes female financial independence and freedom from debt for women—no mom will turn that down! And I just bet the next time the debate arises about who is Mom's "favorite," a quick glance will be shot your way.

- Violet incense has long been considered "happy" incense as it lifts both moods and expectations. A violet plant provides similar positive energies. Four purple African violets placed in the Wealth area (far back left-hand corner of the main floor of the house) brings along a lifted mood and a bolstered bottom line, bringing Mom happily to the nearest ATM with her deposit of your love and her new cash.

LOSING A LOVED ONE

It's really hard for me to go into anyone's home and perform a consultation after they have just lost a loved one. I'm so tuned in to that energy. It's painful and it hurts and there's just no way around it. But as much as we can acknowledge and try to be empathetic to anyone else's loss, we can feel so impotent at those times, almost like there's not much else we can do to help ease the grief. Except witness it. And validate it. And just be there.

I was consulting with a husband and wife of Filipino origin who had this same soul-gripping challenge of getting over their grief at the loss of a loved one. But let's begin at the beginning. I have a particular way I conduct my consults. I take the information from the clients, essentially energy by energy, beginning with the Career area and moving around the Bagua map in a clockwise manner, asking questions and marking their responses. With this couple, when I got around to the Family/Friends/ Ancestors arena, the husband instantly broke into long, heart-rending sobs. He then put his embarrassed head down on his trembling crossed arms on top of their kitchen table and continued to cry for what seemed like a hundred years.

I looked over at his wife for some idea of what had set off this explosion of emotions, but she steadfastly refused to meet my gaze until her husband could compose himself and educate me about his outburst. I sat patiently and painfully waiting, trying to quash the growing lump in my own throat as well. After a long while he straightened himself up and tearfully told me that his mother had died in the Philippines and that he had been unable to say good-bye to her before she passed. To make matters worse, because of inclement weather difficulties, he wasn't even able to make it to her funeral.

I felt so bad for him and also felt, from this tremendous outpouring of grief and guilt, that she must have just died—like three days ago, or maybe even three hours ago. But I was wrong. Way wrong. She had died thirteen years earlier. Thirteen years and he was still carrying around all this heartache and pain. This became one of those times when I really love my mission, my passion, my job, because not only do I have the privilege of being allowed into someone else's private pain but I get to try to help heal that hole as well—just by knowing some critical information that comes to us from the ages.

They called and asked if I would come to their home for dinner. It was a private celebration, as the husband had tried some of the suggestions I left with them (see below), and he now felt that he had been given a new lease on life, one that didn't come with all the guilt and grief attached. He had let go and was moving forward, and it showed in every area of his life. He found a new, better-paying job. His relations with his wife vastly improved. And, most important, he was at peace, because at last he had made same with his self and with his mother.

No matter how you cut it, death is tough. We fear it, we fight it, and we will do most anything to stave it off. But it is, as they say, inevitable, which must be why there are so many practices and customs to help us cope not only with the mourning and grieving part but with the moving on part as well. It's also curious to me that almost every culture's death traditions hold the same three elements: a time accorded to a burial or funeral ceremony, sacred ground to hold the bodily remains, and/or some way of memorializing or honoring the ones who have gone on before us. So since death is as old as time itself, there might not be much that's new here in the way of ritual, but there might just be something inside this information that will bring you that new lease on life after someone you love has passed on.

• At the wake or the funeral, place a photo of the dearly departed in a prominent position for all to see. On the back of this picture, write the loved one's name, date of birth, and date of death and maybe a little paragraph that would describe who this person was, inside and out. You know, was he the class clown always trying for a laugh, or was she so painfully shy that we were all amazed when she married the class clown always trying for a laugh. That sort of thing. Try to put this picture close to the coffin, keeping the energies connected and creating a "space" of honor for the departed. After the ceremony, take this picture home and put it somewhere special and important for forty-nine days (a number that symbolizes redemption and resurrection in many cultures). After the forty-ninth day, put the picture in the Family/Friends/Ancestors area (middle of the left-hand wall on the main floor), where it will, as has been told, cause the family member to smile luck and fortune down on the rest of the clan for the rest of their lives.

• Candles can be continuously burned to help illuminate the way for the soul of the departed to leave one world on its way to the next. Groupings of three green candles (both the color and the number associated with the element of wood, accorded to this Family area) burned with intention creates smoke that quickly releases the spirit onward and upward. At the least, most traditions maintain that two white candles should burn constantly during the funerary rites to help light the way for the newly departed to reach their next level.

• Feng Shui dictates tell us to turn all mirrors inside the house of the deceased around so that they face the other way. This, in fact, reflects beliefs found in other traditions that link the spirit of the departed with mirrors and maintain that they can potentially have distracting or even harmful effects. For those who have passed over from the Jewish, Greek, or other Orthodox faiths, the belief is that mirrors should be covered for at least the first three days after death so that the spirit will move on to the next dimension and not be drawn, attracted, or attached to this one.

· Smoke and flowers both have strong relationships to the spirit world. Ancient custom holds that burning incense helps to release the soul of the loved one and that burning incense next to a vase of a combination of red, yellow, and white flowers will provide a beautifully strewn pathway to the next resting place.

· On the anniversary of the death, loved ones should create some sort of gift for the departed member. In Eastern cultures, a drawing is placed inside a homemade red envelope and then burned so that the smoke carries the spirit or energies of the gift to the intended. Placing flowers on the gravestones of our dearly departed on any special occasion, but particularly on anniversaries, is said to gain the favor of our ancestors.

· Ringing a bell cleans and cleanses any space where grief and BIG emotions might have gathered and makes clear the way for memories to move on.

· The best thing you can do for any loved one who has passed on, in your own efforts to bring them peace, is to find that same space inside yourself. Just breathe. And cry. And know that "this too shall pass" because it will. When the time is right. Give yourself permission to take all the time you need and allow yourself to feel, express, and, yeah, I know I said it before, just breathe.

FATHER'S DAY

How about we skip the silk tie, the obligatory Old Spice, and the Big Bertha driver this year, and we give dear old Dad a little fortune and luck for Father's Day? According to many ancient customs and traditions, Dad is automatically understood to be both breadwinner and head of the household, and with such a huge task at stake, these cures were meant to help with those endeavors and responsibilities. We know that some households have a mom who wears the pants, and even though the premise of Dad doing solely same may sound a tad old-fashioned, you can still bolster your father's fortune and luck by giving the following gifts to bring longevity, prosperity, and happiness to Pop, and, frankly, who deserves those more? Some great gift ideas for the even greater dad:

- A metal-framed mirror (to be hung in the Helpful People/ Travel area of the house—lower right-hand corner of the main floor or office). A mirror hanging here not only brings him his due (or "honor," as they tell it in the ancient texts) but will also strengthen the metal element associated with this area. This will then bring him some of same . . . in the form of silver and gold. Yup, hanging a mirror in this area will bring Dad a better bottom line, the reflective gift that keeps on giving . . . sometimes even to the 401(k).

- In fact, giving Dad anything made from precious metals will quickly manifest some good fortune for him that, if you play your cards right, might just spill over to you. And speaking of playing cards, give Dad the edge in the next poker game by giving him three Chinese coins tied on a piece of red ribbon, string, thread, or yarn. Holding on to this Good Fortune

Coin Cure might also just find him holding the next big winning hand. Putting a pile of coins in this corner brings BIG METAL luck. The more coins the better, so dig into the couch the next time he gets up and move the quarters that just spilled from his pockets over into his corner.

• Portraits of his own ancestors hung in this same space (Helpful People) are said to increase his successes, his influence, and his power. WOW, all good stuff from Grandpa and pals. Portraits of anyone whom Dad respects hung here will empower him and enable him to find his own path a whole lot easier to tread.

• A small statue of a bear (or any image of same) will bring Dad strength, courage, stability, and protection. And there's a big BONUS attached here as according to Feng Shui that very same Smokey will protect the house from fire or robbery if Dad has to travel or be away from home for stretches at a time.

• And when in doubt about how to lift your dad's spirits, bake him a pie. All dads love pie!

GRANDPARENTS DAY

In appointment after appointment after appointment, when I get to the part of a consultation when I talk to my clients about their family of origin, A LOT of times I hear stories filled with recrimination and resentment and outright anger. And then, when I next ask, "Tell me, then, who nurtured you through your childhood?" the answer I almost always receive is the same: "My grandmother" or "My grandfather" or "My father's mother was

Father's Day Apple Pie

(SERVES 6 TO 8)

Prepared or premade pie dough
8 medium-sized baking apples (any kind but
* McIntosh)*
2 tablespoons butter
2/3 cup brown sugar
3 teaspoons cinnamon
1 teaspoon nutmeg
1/2 teaspoon ginger
1 egg, beaten

1. Make the pie dough and set aside.
2. Preheat oven to 375 degrees. Peel, core, and slice the apples. In a bowl, mix the sugar and the spice and everything else nice (your love for Pop—THIS is the secret ingredient) together. Pour this mixture over the sliced apples until they are well coated.
3. Line the bottom of a standard 9-inch baking pan with the dough and fill the pie shell with the apples. Put small pats of butter over the apple mixture and then cover the top with dough. Brush the dough with the beaten egg and loosely cover with aluminum foil before putting in the oven to bake for twenty-five minutes.
4. After twenty-five minutes, remove the foil and continue to bake for another twenty minutes to brown the top of the pie.
5. Allow the pie to cool before serving. Or just give it to Dad and get your own dessert.

always there for me" . . . or . . . "My nana saved my life." On
and on and on.

In my own life, I have a friend who is as close to me as my
own sister. She is one of eight kids—seven boys and my girl,
Patti. Her parents are from Ireland, and even though her dad
passed around the same time that my own parents did (some
twenty years ago), her mom is still known to everyone as "Nan,"
short for Nana. She's everyone's Nan. She has at least a gajillion
grandchildren of her own now, but she still finds time each and
every Christmas to send my own son a twenty-dollar bill and always signs the card, "Love, Nana."

Grandparents are the greatest. They don't care when you cut
school. In fact, they usually are the ones who'll answer the phone
and tell the secretary that you are upstairs in bed with a terribly
high fever. And when you were in bed with that terribly high
fever, one of them was usually there to make sure there was some
flat ginger ale around (WHOEVER MADE THAT CURE UP,
ANYWAY? Oh, right, grandparents!). They put the cool cloth
on your head, put a cool iron on your wrinkled uniform shirt,
and let your friends drink beer in the kitchen so they'd know
how really cool you were.

They know our foibles and our flaws, and they pretty much
absolutely don't care, because they love us, especially when we
come to visit.

Whether your grandparents live close by or are really far away
(yes, Heaven counts, too) we owe them more than we ever actually take time to think about. For better or for worse, this ancestral marriage dictates our genetic makeup from the health of our
heart to the type of our blood and every cellular collaboration in
between. In so many cultures this integration initiates and fosters
an immense degree of reverence and respect, not only for grandparents but for the old and the elderly in general.

Thankfully, there are so many different ways to incorporate rituals and gifts that honor these wise (and, let's face it, sometimes cranky) elders, especially on this, their very own celebration called Grandparents Day. (But keep in mind that we should be honoring them every day of the year because without them, well, we wouldn't be here—that alone is reason enough to stop and take a minute to absorb some ancient ways of bringing modern love to these wonderful folks.)

By far, photos link us more than any other medium and are so important on so many different levels in keeping memories active and alive and keeping the chain linked. But metal isn't applicable for these efforts. Wood, the element most associated with our families and particularly our ancestors, is what we want to frame our pictures in before we place them: Grandma with you sitting on her lap wearing her favorite reindeer sweater that one unforgettable Christmas; or your and Grandpa's favorite fishing photo, the one with the tall tale attached. Display these shots in wooden frames in the Ancestor part of the house (middle of the left-hand wall) and incorporate wisdom, honor, "Descendant's Luck," and grandparent energy into your home and into your life. Here are some specific ways to honor your grandparents and elders:

• Take three pictures of any relatives and place them in separate wooden frames. Nine days before Grandparents Day, light three green candles in front of the three wooden frames with the pictures in them. The green candles heal any ailing ancestry, as green is the color of growth and transformation, and lighting them transports your intentional healing energies to your grandparents. The gift is the three pictures to your grandparents which you present on Grandparents Day. Note that the candles need not burn down completely, but just until the wick meets the wax, and then you can blow them out. This ritual–cum–gift activates not only longevity and luck for them but also Descendant's Luck for you.

• A flower, plant, or floral arrangement is an appropriate gift for grandparents as they represent that sincerity, honesty, perfection, and beauty can be attained only from the growth of

---

Something Special
(to Do with Your Kids)
to Honor the Ages

All children, young and old, love stories, and they especially love stories about people they actually know or know they are related to. Here's a project that anyone can do. It works wonders with kids and their confidence, and will also honor your . . . and their . . . GRANDPARENTS!

Assemble some photos of all grandparents involved. Remember, we don't necessarily just mean blood relatives—in some cases, great-aunts and -uncles count as much as actual grandparents. But you get the picture. Have everyone share and record memories and stories. Record them on a CD or tape or make a collage of pictures while penning a poem or two that describes the bond that glues you all together. Make a whole night of it. Or even schedule times for this whole effort—the second Sunday of the second month of the first full moon. You know, something everyone can look forward to that will always be there to take you back. The whole idea here is to create a record of familial history that will survive long after some of the members involved do. A beautiful project from start to finish.

wisdom. The lotus symbolizes rising from troubled times and becoming stronger, a hearty evergreen plant represents strength, and a peace lily or money plant are also good choices. Bamboo, however, is the best of all as it grants them easy old age and longevity.

• Quick fix energy: to give your grandparents a statue or small picture of a crane is to offer them a healthy and long life, one filled with peace during their longevity. Also, paintings or images of waterfalls attract luck and good fortune.

• When a grandparent is ill, gift him or her with healing energies from your own space by putting a plant in the Family, Friends, and Ancestors area and dedicating the plant to the ailing ancestor. Make this dedication consciously, and nurture and take care of the plant.

4		
Wealth and Prosperity	Fame and Reputation	Relationship, Romance, and Marriage
Family, Friends, and Ancestors	Health	Children and Creativity
Knowledge and Self-Cultivation	Career	Helpful People and Travel

THE PERFECT PLAN of your perfect life (which is, after all, the goal of this book) includes perfect health, perfect love with the perfect partner, and lots and lots of wealth, prosperity, and abundance. But what wealth looks like to one person doesn't necessarily look the same to another. For one, it may mean financial freedom, absolutely no debt of any kind, and a whole host of zeros in a never dwindling bank account. To someone else, wealth may mean facing the dawn of each new day with joy and expectations of all kinds of abundance. To others, wealth may mean contributing something wonderful and beautiful to this world with every bit of self-expression you exude inside every breath you take.

The energy of Wealth is indeed about abundance, but it is also about order, organization, the Universal Laws of Attraction, the ability to receive, and harmony in the home and in every other aspect of your life. Time and time again, philosopher and layman alike have noted that no one can become a true financial success in his life unless he truly loves his life and what he does with it. Why? Because (and history has proven this) no man (or woman) can become abundant in ANY area of his life unless there is order in EVERY area of his life. Money, abundance, prosperity, and riches—all of these aspirations are manifestations of the same energy, but you must be in harmony with these intentions in order to attract those results—otherwise there will most surely be a separation between you and your infinite supply.

The Laws of Attraction state clearly and firmly that you will get what you want when you believe you deserve it and when you know that there is enough for everyone, including and especially you. Intend it and then get ready to RECEIVE it. Next, send your energy to abundance, and not only will it return to you but it will expand all around you—even if "it" is money. And even if today you don't have any at all, open yourself to the Universal supply. Receive with gratitude and love yourself enough to give some of whatever "it" is to others with grace. Your own receptivity, along with your own gratitude, will make it happen—whether it's currently present in your life or not . . . for the moment, pretend you are about to hit it really big! This attitude of expectation then opens the doors and unlocks the way to the Universal vault and allows you a free pass to all the prosperity and wealth you could ever want. Now allow yourself to take that to the bank!

The area of Wealth is located in the far back left-hand corner of your home, bedroom, office, or any other place you spend time, and the color associated with it is purple, the color of kings and emperors. The number that corresponds to this sector is 4, and so a traditional Wealth cure is to put four pieces of amethyst (an abundance-attracting crystal) somewhere inside this space.

CHINESE NEW YEAR

You no longer need to live near any city where there is a large Asian community to know that Chinese New Year has become an event that is almost as widely celebrated among Westerners as the one that falls each year on January 1. But unlike the Western New Year, which is marked by a big ball dropping to welcome in the New Year, the date of the Chinese New Year is not fixed; rather it comes on the first day of the second new moon after the winter solstice . . . now, there's a dim sum mouthful. This new moon and the fifteen days following it are celebrated as the beginning of a new year for people of Asian origin and descent.

Each Chinese New Year also corresponds to one of the animals represented on their astrological, or zodiac, wheel. Therefore, each individual year has its own inherent qualities accorded to that same animal and so will offer associative opportunities and portents as well as feats and feasts, ALL potentially brimming with fortune and luck.

In other words, Chinese New Year is as serious a celebration for Eastern traditions as our New Year celebration is in the West. The holiday spans two weeks, which is the time it takes for the new moon to grow to full. For those of us who are Westerners, however, the holiday provides us with yet another chance to review our resolve and goals (read: our New Year's resolutions!) set for the following twelve months and possibly polish our personal intentions now that we can have a New Year "do-over."

Of course, there is much that the two holidays and cultures share in common. Both New Years are acknowledgments of the beginnings of new cycles and ask people to shed the old and make way for the new. Here are a few more ideas that will make any New Year celebration a success:

- Clean the clutter and then clean some more.

- Wear red clothes (to augur fortune and great good luck).

- Make loud noises at midnight to keep the evil or malign spirits at bay for the whole of the New Year ahead—and on that exact day.

- Try not to use sharp utensils (so as not to cut into your prosperity).

- And eat these special and lucky foods: black-eyed peas and mandarin oranges.

There are also some major but really fun(damental) differences that Asian cultures hold dear to ring in their New Year with Health and Happiness and much, much Prosperity. For example, it is a tradition on the fourth day of the Chinese New Year to create an elaborate meal and acknowledge the bounty that the kitchen continually brings to the table. On day five, these New Year celebrations honor the elders of the family by visiting them and gifting them with a red flowering plant that will immerse them in good fortune. Try to incorporate some of these customs and rites into your own events surrounding the Chinese New Year, and you will double your odds of having one fortuitous and fabulous New Year.

Use some of these other cures to bolster your own lucky intentions:

- Place a bowl of big, fresh, fragrant oranges on your kitchen and/or dining room table to bring health, longevity, and lifted spirits to your year ahead. Orange essential oil has long been recognized as a natural antidepressant as well as an exuberant mood lifter.

- It is customary where climate permits to place a lemon, lime, or orange tree outside the front entryway of your home for the fifteen days of the New Year to invite happiness to come in and stay awhile. Where weather won't allow, you can use fake fruit trees outside.

- Try to pay off some sort of debt during this time, even if you just pay pennies against aging interest on a credit card. This will augur well for future financial gains.

- Giving anyone money during this time of the year, especially inside a red envelope (Eastern tradition says to give children a dollar inside a red joss envelope—you can get these at any Asian market), will also add to your own bottom line— tithing from the traditional Eastern perspective.

• Finally, much the same as our creating resolutions, there is an Eastern custom of writing down one's wishes and dreams in red ink and placing this paper inside a red envelope. On the last day of the New Year full moon, burn the envelope and send your smoke signals for a phenomenal New Year to the Sky Gods. This single action usually seals the deal for your hopes, wishes, and dreams.

• And, as always, GONG XI FA CHI. This axiom says, "May you live in interesting times!"

SALTY FRIDAYS (OR HOW TO CAST YOUR DEBT UPON THE WATERS)

School loans, credit cards, car payments, rent, mortgage, tuition—the list can go on and on. Do any of these concerns cause you sleepless nights and restless days? Do they constantly contribute to stirring up a whole pot of debt? Does this sound familiar? Even writing the word *debt* gives me the willies. Been there and done that. And indeed, I can personally attest to the great success of not one but BOTH of these cures! I truly KNOW that when you believe and then begin to enact these empowering enhancements, the results will start to eat away at the big mountain or little anthill of money you owe. Now you can finally climb to the peak, plant your flag of financial free-dom, and move on to address other, usually more interesting considerations in your life.

One of these get-out-of-debt adjustments works more quickly

than the other, but they both can and will lighten your load and lessen your financial burden. When you make the commitment to perform these rituals as regularly as you plan to pay down your outstanding interest, you will begin to see immediate gratification (a feeling that probably had something to do with putting you in debt in the first place). As mentioned, these cures can be very potent, but it is a critical caveat to remind you that clutter in the home or office can cause the same result on your bottom line. If you are intent on cleaning up your debt, be sure to have that same willpower and do exactly the same thing in the spaces where you live and work. CLEAN THE CLUTTER!

CURE #1: DEBT-FREE FRIDAY . . .
SALTY SLOW SIMMER

For this exercise you will need a container of sea salt, kosher salt, or rock salt, along with the regular salt shaker that you already use in your kitchen.

Then, EVERY Friday, without fail, sometime before eleven AM, add a pinch or two of the sea salt to your regularly used salt shaker. You must visualize, while performing this act, that you are reducing your debt . . . substantially. You must also not question where the money will come from to pay down your debt, but only believe that after repeated times of doing this same ritual, week in and week out, you will find personal financial freedom from debt.

You may be wondering why this cure is enacted on Fridays. This would be one of those instances where the cure is so ancient that the "Why" is remote, but referred to in ancient texts. I like to think that the ancient powers that be chose Friday because now it's traditionally recognized as the day the eagle lands—pay day!

When all debts have been tremendously reduced (to within reasonable and payable proportions) or have been eradicated completely, you can go ahead and stop the ritual.

If you miss or skip a Friday, don't freak. Just continue the next week with the same intentions. If you begin to skip Fridays regularly (and, really, this adjustment isn't that difficult to perform and it really does work), then you have bigger issues than debt on your plate and you may want to consider seeking out someone to help talk you through your fear of becoming financially independent.

CURE #2: DEBT-FREE FRIDAY . . . THE FAST TRACK

If you are really deep in debt and really serious about getting out of it quickly (or if there is danger of impending legal action), then consider rounding up the ingredients for the following recipe. Then cook up a plan that buys you time, and in time will begin to buy you financial independence.

This cure works quickly but requires both your diligence and your dedication.

You will need a few hefty shakes of salt from your kitchen salt shaker along with any red spice powder that you can grab off any local grocery shelf. Cinnabar is the actual ingredient to use with this cure, but it is next to impossible to obtain in the United States and is potentially toxic, so go ahead and use any red spice. You'll also need a small mirror along with two whole, fresh, not yet ripe limes and a plastic container to hold the whole shebang. For my own agenda, I went to an Asian market and just picked up a red spice off the rack, but have recommended to clients who have no access to Asian markets that they can also use paprika. You can find that red spice almost anywhere.

Next, follow these steps:

On any Friday morning, anytime before eleven o'clock, shake some salt from your regular kitchen shaker into the plastic container. About eight shakes should do it. Add a hefty pinch of your red spice powder to this mix.

Then take the mirror and walk the four corners of your home and/or office (or any other space if so inclined) with the express intention of getting out of debt. Stop at each of the four corners of the main floor of the house and tilt the mirror until it actually reflects the corner itself. Do this in the four corners found on the inside of the main floor of your living space.

Next, roll the two unripe limes in the palms of both of your hands for five minutes, all the while visualizing your financial issues flowing from inside your head, heart, body, and soul into the unripened fruit. In essence, the fruit is taking the burden off your hands, so to speak.

Once you're done with this visual exercise, take the now debt-burdened limes and place them into the plastic container with the salt and the red spice powder. Close the container.

Carry this container to any source of moving water (a river, stream, ocean, or lake) and throw the limes over your LEFT shoulder and into the waters.

Then (and this is VITALLY IMPORTANT) close the container (as you will be taking this back home with you) and be sure as you walk away never to look back. Taking the plastic home with you, make sure that only your money worries get carried away—eco-friendly while also ending your relationship with debt.

This ritual has been known to be foolproof when done three Fridays in succession. If you skip a Friday, you must begin again. If you look back or try to track the disposal of your debt, this cure will not work. But if you do mistakenly turn back, you won't turn into a pillar of salt either. If by the second or third

Friday you are still deep in debt, don't let that shake your faith. Wait three weeks and begin the entire process again. You soon will be thinking of new ways to spend your hard-earned cash and everyone you owe will be out of the proverbial way.

1040, GOOD BUDDY . . . TAX DAY . . . APRIL 15

Every week or two they're taken out of your paycheck, as a favor to you, of course. You pay them at the checkout counter with almost every purchase you make, and then, once a year, you're also given the opportunity to pay just a little (or a lot) more to keep this country running smoothly and to keep us all safe. And we pay them so we can all enjoy the freedoms that come with living in the Land of the Free. By now we should all know that we are talking about taxes. Whether personal, property, estate, or otherwise, taxes are as much a part of our lives as is air, the only difference being that air is free and, well, taxes just ain't.

So if the words "the taxman cometh" cause you to think about anything other than an old Beatles song or have you personally singing the blues, let's blow that angst, anxiety, and angina right off the calendar and show you ways to bring some big bucks into your bankbook. As long, of course, as you pay your taxes on all the new monies that these next cures will carry to you.

HEALTHY, WEALTHY, AND WISE

- Three I Ching or gold Chinese coins (the Good Fortune Coin Cure) strung together on a piece of red ribbon (string, thread, or yarn) and kept inside your wallet and affixed to the back of the front-entry door handle (on the inside) will improve personal profits immediately.

- Sprinkle ginger on your checks, your cash, and all your coins. This is a traditional way to spice up your bottom line. Or put one hundred coins in a silver box and place this in the Helpful People area (front, or bottom, right-hand corner of home or office), and start to cash in on this cure.

- Any basket of fresh fruit or flowers kept on the kitchen or dining room table, for increased abundance, will garner great gifts and prosperity. An orchid, particularly a purple one, placed with intent on the dining room table will garner great gifts of wealth and authority.

- Place a fountain of moving water either right outside or immediately inside the front entryway of your home or office. Moving water is an excellent way to conduct a flow of abundance straight into your house. Make sure, if the fountain is inside, that the water is flowing INTO the home and not out the door, lest that's where your opportunities will go as well.

- You can also generate an outrageous income by placing a fountain of moving water inside the Wealth area of your home or office (remember, no moving water in the bedroom!). Place the fountain in the far back left-hand area of the main floor and add some additional ooomph by adding four purple amethyst crystals to this water, piled one atop the other to create a "mountain" of wealth.

- Place a jade, bamboo (with four stalks), or money plant in the Wealth corner of your home or office. Eastern cultures rank jade as the most precious of all gems. As well, the Chinese character for jade also represents the number 3, so we have heard tell that to nurture this plant in that area will triple your wealth in one-third the time.

- Bringing three fresh, vibrant rosemary plants into the kitchen is said to bring along with them healthy financial independence, especially for women. However, ANY three plants added to the kitchen decor will also significantly add to the amount available to you at the ATM.

- Painting your front door RED is a standard and classic wealth cure in Feng Shui. This entrance to all of life's opportunities includes bringing bundles of cash your way as well. If you cannot paint your front door red, simply try gold, yellow, or green—whichever will match your home's decor. If you simply cannot or will not change the color of your front door, then paint a small red dot (you can even use red nail polish) at your eye level on the left side of the doorjamb of your front entryway. This little dot has big fortunate implications.

THE FIRST NEW MOON IN ARIES, OR THE COSMIC TREASURE MAP

In our culture, the astrological sign associated with the ram, the one called Aries, is also considered the first sign of the zodiac and therefore is thought to be the beginning of a brand-new astrological year. So, just to be clear here, we have January 1, the traditional start of the Western New Year; then we have the second new moon after the winter solstice, creating a space on the yearly calendar to celebrate the Chinese New Year, usually sometime in early to mid-February; and following that, just as the crocuses are creeping through the fresh mulch laid down for the first days of spring, comes the advent of the zodiacal New Year represented by the first new moon in Aries. This date generally falls early in April. So really we have four months in which to put our ducks in a row and get quacking on what our "NEW" Year should, would, and could look like. Whew! How lucky is that?

So what can you do on this zodiacal New Year? I have learned something powerful, empowering, and almost completely magical that you can enact when that first new moon arrives in Aries, something that can make your wildest dreams come true, and all this while you are still wide awake. It's called Treasure Mapping and consists of creating a collage of clarity that adds power, visualization, passion, and personal goal setting to your hopes, wishes, and dreams, no matter how far-fetched or wild they may be.

I have literally hundreds of Treasure Mapping client anecdotes that I could share with you to show the power of this one truly simple exercise, but I'll pick just two to convince you that with little more effort than it takes to cut out your negative attitude while cutting representations (i.e., pictures) of your perfect life out of magazines and catalogs, you can make your dreams come true. This creative tool has been around for ages, and, as you'll see soon, there's a good reason why!

My client Carolyn was familiar with Treasure Mapping, but she had never done the exercise using Feng Shui as a guide nor had she ever heard about starting the map on the new moon in Aries to assure quick and easy success. She's a singer and actress, and her goal was to get a role in a Broadway play. But she's not really a dancer and she's not really that young anymore, and her optimism for this dream was beginning to fade along with her passion and enthusiasm. She took on a variety of sales jobs to see her through financial needs, but she also acted in community theater to continually keep a hand in her chosen craft. When I met her, Carolyn was getting ready to throw in the theatrical towel and move on to something "safer" that would secure her future a bit more.

I met her in February and told her to get nine legal-size envelopes and label each one with the nine different Feng Shui energies represented in our own navigational treasure map called the Bagua. Besides enacting certain Feng Shui cures and adjustments inside her living space, I also counted on her to empower her own intentions by creating this all-important collage of her hopes and dreams. I told her that whenever she had the time and/or the inclination, to go ahead and cut out pictures, depictions, words, and symbols that represented her goal of being part of a Broadway cast. I then told her that on the first new moon in Aries, she should begin to construct this collage—even if she affixed or glued only one picture in place on that day. But, and this is equally important, she needed to complete the entire Treasure Map by the next full moon (full moons are traditionally a time of fruition and endings in astro-speak). She also needed to follow the clockwise directions of the energies represented on the Feng Shui Bagua map (see page xxiv for Bagua map). So, for example, anything symbolizing Wealth for her should be put in the upper left-hand corner of her collage. In her Fame area, top center, she should put any photos or representations of other famous Broadway actors/plays so they could act as a beacon and inspiration for the opportunities that she now could expect to come knocking.

Sometimes our Higher Powers really do work in mysterious ways. That June, Carolyn called to tell me that she had decided to take a job selling time-shares in Florida. However, when she got to La Guardia Airport, her flight had been delayed indefinitely due to bad weather. She ended up seated next to a husband-and-wife "team," with the wife headed to Chicago and the husband off to Atlanta. But, of course, no one was going anywhere while wind gusts and rain blasts were having their way. Carolyn and the couple got to talking, and it turned out, and I swear this is true, that they were BOTH Broadway agents and were going their separate ways to look for some talent to tap for a new play that they had been hired to cast. Carolyn got one of those jobs! She was then introduced to a producer who hires actors and actresses to entertain on his cruise ships, and to this day Carolyn is busy traveling everywhere, acting every day, and truly loving her life.

The second story is mine. It's short but it is very sweet. After five years of infertility and just as many miscarriages, I learned about mapping, using Feng Shui, and the first new moon in Aries. I carefully constructed a barrage of babies and their accoutrements all over my board. Did it work? My healthy, smart, and happy son just turned eleven.

FINDING THE PERSONAL POT OF GOLD: YOUR TREASURE MAP

1. Use any piece of poster board, large or small paper, or even a corkboard. Cover the whole thing (front and back if you want) with pictures, symbols, and words representing your hopes, wishes, and dreams. Put all appropriate symbols in the same places as the corresponding energies would go on the tic-tac-toe–style Bagua map, saving the biggest goals for the center.
2. In fact, put a picture of YOU that YOU love in the middle of this board.
3. Use verbal affirmations as you create your visual ones. Keep the map somewhere you can see it daily to remind you of what's just around the corner.

4. Any leftover pictures, affirmations, words, or symbols should be kept inside a box of some sort (this can be a shoebox, one made of wood, or even one included with your family's sterling silver). Keep cutting out inspirational ideas to add to this box. If something or someone on your map manifests or becomes less ideal than you once thought, it's okay to paste or tape another visual over that picture, but don't get too carried away with this idea.

5. Each new moon in Aries should find you updating your treasure map, reflecting your updated desires. Bless that which has manifested for you and think about what has not and whether you truly need what you asked for as an attendant energy in your life. And remember, just because you put the picture of the Porsche in the Wealth area doesn't necessarily mean this didn't work if you're not driving down the Autobahn next to a Ferrari by the summer. If your current car payment was reduced by any amount of money, your manifesting map was working in your favor.

	5	
Wealth and Prosperity	**Fame and Reputation**	Relationship, Romance, and Marriage
Family, Friends, and Ancestors	Health	Children and Creativity
Knowledge and Self-Cultivation	Career	Helpful People and Travel

SOMETIMES WHEN I speak in public or I go to a client's house, they tell me to "go ahead and just skip the Fame area," because they believe these energies have to do ONLY with professions that require you to be highly recognized—such as writers, models, actors, singers, politicians, or any other public persona. They don't want to be on *Oprah,* they say. I tell them not to worry, I'll take care of that one myself. Then I explain that, like every single one of the energies represented on our navigational Bagua map, this thing called Fame also speaks to how you are recognized by others in your family, your community, and the world at large. It's not only about being on the cover of *Redbook* magazine (again, stay tuned, I'm working on that one, too) but also about little Johnny or Mary saying a big "THANK YOU" for getting the stuff for the school science fair with one day left to spare.

In essence, Fame is about recognition, reward, and appreciation—for your efforts, no matter what field you are in. It is about acknowledgment for your actions, gratitude for your goodness, and well-deserved reward and respect for your contributions, whether you are pointing to a new Pontiac on *The Price Is Right* or you have just read the latest Nora Roberts to your cancer-ridden next-door neighbor. Fame might be fleeting, but your reputation stands forever.

According to the energies associated with this sector, personal empowerment and transcendence define this space at its apex and its best. Changes happening both inside and out that will make you a better person—better than you already are—just by the flip of the Fame switch. Speaking of switches: To energize and activate the energies and opportunities associated with this arena, think bright lights (even if you don't want your name up in them), sun or moon motifs, anything triangular, and especially anything on fire or red in color. Burning up the charts, heating up your Q factor, fanning the flames of reputation and reward— are you sensing the theme here? Shoot for the moon, end up swinging on a star, or maybe become one yourself.

Fame and Reputation is located in the back middle, or center space, of your home, bedroom, office, or any other place you spend time. The element associated with the Chi of Fame is fire and the color ascribed to both Fame and Reputation (a place of personal integrity as well as personal safety) is red. The number that heats up this area is the magic number 9, the integer that represents completion, fruition, and the attainment of all your personal ideals and goals. In almost every numerological tradition it is considered to be THE most important number. Now that you have all this valuable information, you'll be able to become one burning hot tamale.

HAPPY NEW YEAR!

Wishing you a New Year filled with FORTUNE and LUCK! Only now, lucky you, I tell you how to make that happen.

Resolution revolution! Oh, right, we say we're going to start to exercise, lose weight, and improve our diets, our relationships, our kids' study habits, as well as our own drinking ones. We're going to change to better jobs, be more philanthropic, and, as usual, get back in touch with all of those who require a return call from six months ago as time seems, minute by warped minute, to speed out of control. We rush here and there and then believe that just because this one single day declares that you can change your whole life inside a singular twelve-month span, that could actually ever happen. As if!

Now, don't get me wrong. I certainly ascribe and subscribe to the belief that if we create an intention, follow it with an empowering action, and trigger or activate that same intention, then we WILL most definitely see positive results. The difference is that if you are still in the same-size jeans, or still doing the same job, and still reaching for the Pinot Noir after you have created a platform to change those behaviors AND after you have enacted some of these Lucky Day adjustments, well, then, there needs to be more of an internal assessment and less of the hanging of the wind chimes in the middle of the kitchen while eating on black plates with a white shirt on because that will help you shed those last twenty pounds (no kidding!).

So try ANY or ALL of these cures to make this (or any) New Year your best one ever. But really, just deciding that this will be YOUR year and taking a couple of these intentional actions to provide that should be just the golden ticket (and I mean that proverbially, so put the Wonka bar back in the kids' candy cabinet and get on your stationary bike, the one you gave yourself for Christmas!).

As you will see, some of this stuff needs to happen just prior to actual New Year's Day, either before or on New Year's Eve in some cases. My advice is just to read through these cures before you hand-pick what resonates with you and your resolutions. Then scratch the bottom of the bunch, and go to the top of the class and learn some New Year Shui. HAPPY NEW YEAR now becomes redundant!

- One of the most powerful cures for a power-packed New Year is practical as well. Your entire house, or as much as possible, should be cleaned before New Year's Day. This will clear the way for new and exciting energies to enter your life immediately. You should NEVER, though, clean the house on New Year's Day itself, as this is thought to "sweep" away all the Fortune and Luck that is headed your way for the coming year. If you find that you cannot address your entire space, then simply concentrate on the kitchen, as this is the one space inside your environment that represents your Health, Happiness, and Prosperity—Three Great Blessings that will lead to one spectacular New Year.

· The Feng Shui New Year "Gold Standard" is to move twenty-seven things around your home on New Year's Day and watch as Fortune and Luck invade your life from every direction. Moving twenty-seven things is harder to do than you might think, but remember, it will also count if you just move the salt and pepper shakers so they sit on the other side of each other. The object here is to change it up. Then you'll find the same old, same old heading out with the old year.

· Refill your sugar reserves (canisters, bowls, whatever) to restock your supply and ensure a sweet year ahead.

· Anytime immediately prior to New Year's Day, take a trip to the ATM and pull some cold cash out of your account. Get a good, hearty smattering of small bills and put them inside your wallet, making it appear stuffed full and fat. This simple tip will bring you untold and unexpected fortunes in the year ahead. If you want to get really magical, put twenty-seven one-dollar bills in your wallet and forty-nine coins in your change purse. Then sprinkle dried ground ginger inside and outside of same (go ahead and get inspired and sprinkle the ginger on the money, too) and amble over and give a little shake onto your checkbook, too. Then think about me when you're out buying that new Persian rug, okay?

- As Tom Hanks reminded us in the movie *A League of Their Own,* "There's no crying in baseball," and the same thing holds true on New Year's Day. Tradition says that crying on this day can trigger a deluge that ends up seeing you cry the whole year long. Also, try not to lose your temper, use foul language (uh-oh . . . careful there, Ellen), or whine. In fact, we are taught that the VERY FIRST words uttered to you at the top of any New Year will have a HUGE impact on your Fortune and Luck in the twelve months following. If I'm not planning on being home at exactly the stroke of midnight, I bring the proverbial script and pick a person to say those most important three little words to me at midnight. In my case, they're "Health, Happiness, and Prosperity," although I wouldn't stop anyone from using those other three little words, "I love you." Any of the entries from this lexicon will work equally well for all of us.

- If you are at home as the year turns, then open up all the doors and windows, if even for a moment, no matter how chilly, to let the previous year's energies move out and some new interesting ones come in. Also in line with burning off the old and welcoming the new comes the tradition of lighting firecrackers or making noise by banging pots and pans together. This is said to scare away any maligning influences that may have been headed your way.

- On New Year's Day itself, never refer to anything in the past. Instead, talk only of your hopes, wishes, and dreams for the future. Then place nine mandarin oranges in a bowl in your kitchen or on your dining room table to help orchestrate sweet treats that will make the coming year's dreams come true.

- It is considered very auspicious if the first thing you see on New Year's Day is a red bird. If you don't think a red bird will just happen to fly past your window on its way home from the Swallow Jägermeister New Year's Eve party, then get proactive and cut out a picture of a red bird(s) and place it somewhere you will easily see on New Year's Day. (P.S. Magpies, specifically red ones, are known to wing good special benefits your way!)

Chew on This

Many traditions maintain that you should not eat any meat on New Year's Day, as abstaining from this particular food group will then grant you a long and happy life. Also, you are NEVER supposed to use anything sharp (as in knives or scissors) on this same day as this could conceivably cut your coming fortunes in half.

Eating fish on this auspicious day is said to aid in intelligence as well as build immunity while bringing the added bonus of symbolizing a year swimming in abundance and prosperity. And most of the time you can cut and eat it with a spoon (think tuna salad, or cured salmon on a bagel). All through New Year's Day, your house should stay brightly lit with bowls of oranges, fruits, nuts, and candy spread throughout to augur sweet tidings, good health, and lots and lots of happiness for the year ahead. Some cultures even believe the combination of salmon, cabbage, and oranges, eaten as a festive meal on New Year's Eve, is a surefire guarantee to great good fortunes served up every day of the coming year.

Lucky Foods to Start the Year Off Right!

Blini or boxed pancake mix
Crème fraîche or sour cream
Nova, or smoked, salmon
Capers (a spoonful or to taste)
Chopped onions (to taste)

Make the blinis (these are small pancakes about 1 inch in diameter) and let cool. Just before serving, place a dollop of crème fraîche or sour cream on each blini, add the smoked or cured salmon (two pieces do nicely), and finish off with capers and chopped onions to taste. This completes not only a delicious and delightful but also a very fortunate and lucky little meal.

Savoy Cabbage Minestrone

(SERVES 2 TO 4)

This delightful, zesty soup can (and should) be made a day in advance of New Year's Day so you don't have any chopping or slicing to do!

4 tablespoons olive oil
2 leeks, trimmed and chopped
1/2 teaspoon rosemary

8-ounce can chopped tomatoes
Salt and pepper to taste
6 1/2 cups Savoy cabbage, cut into strips
1/2 cup long-grain rice
1 tablespoon Parmesan cheese, freshly grated

1. Heat 1 tablespoon of olive oil in a pan with $\frac{1}{2}$ cup water,

2. Add the leeks and rosemary, and cook over low heat for 10 minutes or until the leeks have softened.

3. Add the tomatoes, season with salt and pepper, and cook for another 10 minutes.

4. Stir in the cabbage, add 4 cups of warm water, increase the heat to medium, and simmer for about 15 minutes.

5. Bring to a boil, add the rice, and stir and cook for about 18 minutes, until tender.

6. Let cool and then store in the refrigerator. On New Year's Day, heat the soup, then ladle it into a tureen and sprinkle with the Parmesan. Serve hot and heat up your good Luck and Fortune.

Spinach and Mandarin Orange Salad

(SERVES 2 TO 4)

Again, if you make the dressing ahead of time, you can enjoy this sweet salad on New Year's Day!

2 tablespoons rice wine vinegar
1 tablespoon orange juice

2 tablespoons olive oil

1/2 teaspoon sugar

1 teaspoon sea salt

1/2 teaspoon freshly ground black pepper

1/4 cup small diced red onion

1 small can sliced mandarin oranges

2 pounds fresh spinach, washed and dried

In a large salad bowl, add the rice wine vinegar, orange juice, olive oil, sugar, salt, pepper, red onion, and orange segments. Mix well, then add the spinach, making sure that all the leaves are touched. Serve cold or at room temperature.

GETTING A RAISE SHUI

You work hard and most nights you're the last one to leave the office. You're efficient and can be counted on and almost always have all the right answers even when the questions seem wrong. Let's face it: You and I both know that you deserve it. I'm talking about a raise and/or promotion, that is. But then that niggling little voice in the back of your head starts in: "What about Jack? There's only so much profit to pass around and he's in here almost as much as I am." Or maybe, like my own graphic artist, Sarah, you are a complete and total genius, just brilliant at your work, and you quietly go about your daily business while contributing greatly to the bottom line of your firm, but you never quite see those billable hours transform into a sizable increase in your paycheck. Of course, Sarah has seen steady increases in her duties and responsibilities, but in her salary? Not so much. Slow, steady, and really, really smart might win the race, but will it get you the raise? Sometimes, when life is fair, then, yes, that might be enough. But there's certainly nothing wrong with having a little (okay, a HUGE) energetic advantage when it comes to getting what YOU DESERVE.

Because that's what the following cures are all about: receiving what you deserve. Sure, sure, Getting a Raise Shui is also about the money because naturally your income should increase when your Q factor does as well. But this is also really about getting the reward you've rightly earned, getting the recognition you've rightly deserved, and enjoying the ride while you are at it. So now that we're all on the same page, let's see how some of you may add another zero to your pay stub while others may simply find their way out the office door, where more opportunity awaits on the other side. Because it's time. Because your talents and your gifts and your time will be far more favored, recognized, and rewarded somewhere else. And because it really is true that when one door closes, another one flies fully open.

Either way, this is what I know from many years of both consulting AND personal experience: If you perform the adjustments that you are about to read, then they will enhance your reputation in your chosen field or profession as well as allow all around you to honor the integrity you bring to your community. They will also validate that you are a valued and valuable addition to your neighborhood, whether that's in a ranch house sitting behind third base of a ball field or in a mega-mansion because you cover the bases as a five-gajillion-dollars-a-year pitcher for the Yankees. These cures are about what you are worth, and what you should earn while actively creating wonderful opportunities to keep you expanding into your dream future.

However, keep in mind that the key to your Lucky Day Getting a Raise Shui cure begins initially in your mind. You need to really believe, deep down inside, that you are worthy of the raise, have earned the recognition, and that the amazing review or the dream-job opportunity heading your way in the NEAR future truly belongs only to you. Okay, enough about that. Now let's do this:

- Take ten minutes and visualize what a great performance on the job you've been doing. As you are rewarding yourself for your own efforts, take four deep breaths in through the nose and exhale them out through the mouth, all the while thinking about and thanking YOU for your own brand of genius and creativity.

- Standing at the door to your bedroom, in your mind's eye, make the room as close to a square or rectangle as it can get. Then divide the room into a tic-tac-toe board, approximately nine smaller sectors inside the one room (sound familiar? Yes, it's the Bagua map; see page xxiv for further info).

- Locate the bottom, middle, and then top center sectors of the bedroom (what would relate to both Career and Fame, respectively, in the Bagua). In both of these spaces, you are going to need to use a chair or stepladder to get to the ceiling.

- Starting with the bottom center Career sector of your bedroom, stand on the stepladder and measure three inches down from the ceiling. Affix a small, round mirror in that specific spot.

- Now move across the room to the reciprocal space (top middle sector of your room, the Fame *gua*). Once again, step on the ladder, measure three inches down from the ceiling, and affix another small round mirror there.

- Try as closely as possible to create a direct effect with these mirrors: They should look like they are stationed directly across from each other and almost reflect each other.

- While you are sticking these small mirrors across from each other on the bedroom walls, you should also be repeating the inferred mantra we started out with: "respect, reward, recognition." Say these three words a total of nine times with the placement of each of the mirrors.

The surefire combo of your accomplishments plus the accolade energy created by positioning the mirrors on those walls will be certain to make you get that promotion or total job change you've been hoping, wishing, and WORKING so hard for!

Fail-safe Flowers to Grow Respect and Reward

In many traditions, flowers are thought to be Spirit made manifest. Since that's the case, my own spirit can't keep mum about what that particular plant can bring to you immediately in terms of Fame and Reputation. Let me share with you a short story about how a beautiful yellow mum worked wonders.

Early on, I had a television agent who sort of floated around his agency. Talented, hardworking, and really handsome, John had recently been promoted from assistant agent to full-fledged-agent status—and this was all great because we had done enough Feng Shui in his little cubicle to practically get him elected to his talent agency board. The problem was there was no office space for J. So, even though he had received the recognition, there wasn't a spare chair, telephone, or an extra four walls to go along with his promotion!

Then one day, an e-mail from John popped into my inbox saying that he had finally gotten the office, but, unfortunately at that moment, not the cash to go along with the couch. My feeling was that the agency thought they could mollify him with the "promotion" and the office space and simply forget about the Franklins. I reminded him, again, that if he wanted the money, the respect, and the room he had to do this: place a YELLOW chrysanthemum in the Fame area of his home or office or anyplace where he spent significant time. Putting that particular color mum into this space would help grow his reputation and his riches exponentially and tremendously—and, equally and importantly, this will do the same for you. This is staple tried-and-true Feng Shui.

Needless to say, John got his bonus, we both shared the credit, and the Korean florist on the corner got a new bunch of yellow mums for all the other agents wanting out of their cubicles.

(If you are in a cubicle or have no space inside your office to place this plant, then get a picture of a yellow mum or even place a package of seeds in this same space for the same result.)

October 9—A Day to Remember

In the Eastern traditions, they believe that you should purchase a yellow mum on the ninth day of October and nurture
it (keep it alive) for twenty-seven days. The plant should be
placed either in the Fame sector on the back wall of your
home or office, or, additionally, on the top center of your desk.
The staunch belief is that if you do this, then you will quickly
rise to a prestigious position of high ranking. Usually I remember this sensational and fast-acting cure only after October is
over, but this year, for sure, I'll remember, and then my mantra
will be "Top of the World, Ma, Top of the World!"

FAME-OUS INTENTIONS

Respect, reward, recognition (we've said it before but it bears repeating)—this should be your single and consistent mantra as
YOU pave the way to your own personal success, great and
good fortune, and, of course, Fame in all of your efforts.

Getting more money for doing their job is paramount in
the panoply of reasons people call for my services and consultations. They come to hear me speak and then quietly come
behind the scenes to ask if they can raise their income, all the
while activating positive energies involved with their jobs.
Their quietness is part hesitation. Why? They somehow think
that if they ask for more money for doing a better job, they
will have to sacrifice something more important in trade.
What I tell them is simple: Any advice I offer here should,
without fail, complement, NOT cancel out, the other. You can

have respect, reward, and recognition—and still love the work you do!

Using one or more of the ancient customs and traditions that follow can bring new birth to your duties in addition to your dollars. The power inherent in the advice given here can actually create a sterling reputation where before there was none. It can even make clear that the access to your ideas can be taken oh so seriously by the BIG brass, where before you were quite possibly considered only part of the chorus—maybe even second-string at that.

Speaking of being part of the chorus, I have a client named Rosie who is from Russia and paints nails for a living. She works at a prestigious salon and is not only highly requested for her exquisite services but highly paid for them as well. Her client-based tips alone afford her a luxurious lifestyle, and she absolutely loves what she does. So, why, then, did she actually engage me? When I was consulting with her it turned out that she was a Russian folksinger in her homeland, but came here with her American husband, who was serving in the military. She found no work in the United States in her beloved field, so she learned the "art of the nail" and went to work honing and filing her craft until she rose to the top. But she still dreams of singing her native music and getting paid for it—not only getting paid, but recognized in that industry as well.

File this, I told her, and then let me know the outcome:

Go to the room that you sleep in (you'd be surprised how many clients I have who don't actually sleep in their "master" bedroom; the mate snores, the traffic outside the window is too loud—whatever. I've learned to do this specific cure in the room that you sleep in, otherwise you risk doing it in the "wrong" room) and locate all the corners in the room. Some have the standard four, and some have more or possibly even fewer, depending on the shape and the architecture of the room.

In each of the corners of the bedroom, hang a red string (the color of Fame energies) from ceiling to floor. Now I have to add a codicil here, which I know from the client archives as well as from personal experience: You *cannot* just take red ribbon, string, thread, or yarn and measure ONE corner and then cut all four (if that's the number of corners in the room) pieces of this red string, according to the one corner you've actually measured out. Houses settle, which changes the architecture, sometimes making the corners uneven. You MUST measure each corner individually, lest you waste three pieces of string and a whole bunch of your own time. It's not worthwhile to cut corners!

These strings now symbolize the columns that are said to hold up the canopy of heaven, while connecting your energies to earth. I was taught that they act as a sort of cosmic phone line to the Heavens, the kind that doesn't drop the call and has no static on the line—kind of like when you call the head of the Russian Embassy in Washington to see if they can intercede with the Russian orchestra to get you an audition (uh-oh, am I spoiling the ending to manicurist Rosie's story?).

You can see what the idea is here: You are asking for a little help from the really BIG brass, bigger than the ones who sit in the corner offices with the great views in the building you work in. You are indeed invoking the help of the Heavens to intercede on your behalf and put you on the road to respect, recognition, and reward.

But first, a little fine-tuning. Back to the strings: At the halfway point on those strings, exactly at that midway between ceiling and floor, fasten another nine-inch red string that will symbolize or represent you and your "Fame-ous Intentions." It helps if you keep reminding yourself—respect, recognition, reward . . . respect, recognition, reward—oh, and remember, you can use this Universal calling card to signal for any life dilemma—just use the color string that is associated with the Chi, or energy, that you would like enhanced. (New partner? Think pink. New job? Think black. Better health? Yellow. Okay, you get it.)

Rosie hung the red string while hanging around waiting for the Russian Embassy to call back. Speaking of which, she's now on her fourth callback with the orchestra, and things are humming along nicely. In Russian, of course.

FOURTH OF JULY (OR THE PATRIOT'S GUIDE TO FASHION)

Oh say, can you see, by the dawn's early light, just exactly what will make you look hot, hot, so sizzling hot, on Independence night? In July, there are three colors that immediately jump to mind that also keep us hoping and hopping all around the concepts of freedom, peace, and independence. Of course, I'm referring to you being the star while earning your own stripes and wearing red, white, and blue. All three of these different colors carry their own specific vibrations that will send a subtle message to everyone around you whenever you wear them. It's like sending a txt msg, except these messages are subliminal and come from your clothes, not your Chocolate or RAZR. And now you might even want that phone in red, because the combo of these three colors, with the fiery, passionate red dominating, will make you number ONE in everyone's five!

Red is the most exciting and vibrant of all the colors in this Feng Shui world and beyond. It can also pump up your own personal energy levels while you wear it, so you can leave the Red Bull at home while you're out cavorting in this hue. Your adrenaline will spike, as will your connection to whomever has the good fortune to come along with you while you are on fire. It's been said that even looking at the color red will stimulate your will to survive. I share all of this with you only to prove the phenomenal, powerful, and potent effect of this specific color.

And now let's get to the important stuff: Wearing red conjures passion and desire, both-feet-off-the-ground sizzle, while creating opportunities for romance and love to join in these heated fireworks. Even wearing a pair of sexy red undies (and who would know but you?) can bring on some pretty steamy days and nights, particularly during this pretty steamy month. Do please keep in mind if you are in need of a little R&R, leave the red back at home in the closet with the cool new kicks.

Then there is the color white. This is the angel to that little red devil. From a spiritual perspective, white says simplicity, purity, and tranquillity. White cools down the heat and fire you've started by wearing arousing red. When too many red nights leave you feeling a little burned out, and you need to tap some inner peace and stall the storms that life sometimes presents, take a break and don something simple, light, and white. Ahh, which is exactly why it's the perennial preferred summer color —now, isn't this cool, to lower the temperature with what you wear?

Finally comes the color blue, the most peace-filled color on the palette, and one that imparts a healthy dose of harmony and healing. Any hue of blue carries a quality that is both refreshing and optimistic at the same time and actually has the distinction of being able to inspire the wearer. It's vibratory rate carries communication as its gift, so what better color to wear if you're a tad shy but want to talk to that special someone (especially if it happens to be a boss, a potential new partner, or even a whole group waiting for you to join in a holiday fireworks celebration, for example)? Wear blue to open your power and your purpose.

Clearly a display of Fourth of July fashion wearing these three colors together won't confuse, but will, on the other hand, allow you a whole host of opportunity to explode individually in the crowd.

A LEG UP ON THE COMPETITION

If the Little Engine That Could ever looked into a train-length mirror, he would certainly have doubted whether he really, really could after all. Who among us hasn't had a bit of bluster when talking about our sport, creative art, or any other performance-oriented accomplishments? I don't care if that's on the golf course, in the symphony hall, or with the blue ribbon blueberry pie you entered in the state fair Bake-Off. There's a reason why fishermen have the last laugh about the one that got away. But we tell the tall tale anyway and hope that it's not only believable but true! Eventually the day will come when we have to prove our prowess, and with that a good dose of confidence can sometimes prove our best coach and our closest ally.

Look, I could tell you a million ways to incorporate luck into your strategies. After all, Vijay has his lucky quarter in his sock and Tiger always wears the same red shirt on the Sunday of whatever tournament he's playing in. In fact, in sports, lucky talismans are legendary. But the lucky penny on the dashboard of Dale Earnhardt's car didn't do much good on that tragic Sunday. So let's not focus as much on what's on the outside as that which is waiting to be born from within.

It's not the "thing" you have on you that will carry the day; it's the expectation of your performance hitting the right note, the home run, or winning the blue ribbon for your blueberry pie. It's all in the preparation and the training and then the belief in yourself. After all is said and done, it's only about how you feel about your best efforts that really matters. Unless you just have to have the biggest-mouthed bass, or the legendary green jacket, or the ring, and then tell everyone on national television that you're going to Disney World—on the team's dime. Before you head to Florida, though, you need to take a little head trip first. There's no packing involved.

- Breathe in through the nose and out through your mouth. Four times. Fifteen seconds between each breath. Pull in a deep, DEEP breath that fills your belly. All the while visualize a white bubble above your head and "see" whatever it is that would be the perfect outcome. Is it you earning the cup at the French Open, or you getting the French onion soup at the head table at the country club because your foursome just won the annual doubles tournament?

- Hold the breath in for a few seconds. Create the visual above your head in a white bubble. Then blow the breath back out through your mouth (like whistling), but (and here's the twist) blow this Chi, or energy, HARD into the picture in the bubble.

- Wait fifteen seconds and do it again. Don't change the visual— keep it constant. Do this four times, waiting fifteen seconds before taking the next breath. Nice and easy does it there, winner.

- You can do this as often as you like prior to and during your event. It will, without question, give you an edge on the competition, and I know this because, well, I think you can, I think you can, I think you can . . . actually, I KNOW you can.

Acquiring (or Replenishing) Activity Chi

This is one very simple bathing exercise that will not only help revitalize your inner reserves but also strengthen your physical, mental, and emotional Chi, or energies. Run a hot bath and add a cup and a half of Epsom salts. Add to this nine pieces of nine different orange rinds or skins. Each piece of rind from each orange should be at least the size of a quarter or a Super Bowl ring. (You can juice the rest of the fruit to give you some nutritional advantages here as well.) Then add seven different flowers (it doesn't matter what kinds of flowers, but preferably they should all be fragrant) to this bath. And remember, if you use roses of any kind, be sure to remove the thorns. Then settle in for a Chi-enhancing soak.

Do this anytime you need an extra boost before going to do battle. There will be a spring in your step, a bloom in your cheek, and a peak in your performance, particularly if you peek into your winner's visual that is a bubble not in this bath but a winning one sitting over your head.

REBIRTH OF A SALESMAN, OR SELL THE SHUI OUT OF IT!

The power of the Fame sector simply cannot be underestimated or, conversely, overvalued enough. Had Willy Loman had this information (and maybe any serotonin-uptake antidepressants), his sons might have been able to stick around to receive quite the inheritance once the death of their salesman pop finally did roll around. This next story will not only attest to that fact but also inspire anyone who might still be the least bit skeptical about the efficacy of letting your own light shine, while getting a little (or A LOT of) help from nine red candles, the strictest gold standard of Fame adjustments. And because some of you may still be a touch skeptical regarding Feng Shui (especially the guy I'm just about to tell you about), it particularly pleases me to recount this next story.

Phyllis (real name used with her enthusiastic permission!) called me with a story that truly touched my heart and immediately pulled me in to try my very best to help 100,000 percent. Not that I don't always offer this same verve and vigor, but Phyllis and her elderly husband were in such dire, and I mean dire, need of some special and fast fortune, I felt especially compelled and compassionate. During that first phone call, Phyllis explained that she and Jim (Phyllis was seventy-four and Jim eighty years young at the time) had been taken to the cleaners and lost absolutely everything they had earned over sixty years of hard work and big dreams. This disaster had just occurred during their well-deserved retirement at the hands of an unscrupulous accountant who thought their life savings would be better served buying him a condo in the Bahamas than supporting them during the latter part of their lives. In short, although the accountant was caught, convicted, and is presently serving out the latter part of his days in a well-deserved stint in the slammer, it didn't put any savings back into Jim and Phyllis's completely (and totally!) depleted bank account.

When Phyllis called she was at the end of her rope and asked if I could waive my normal hourly fee (and wave my magic wand!) and get them on my calendar immediately. I did all three. When I got to their home, they told me that the only way out of this financial fiasco for them would have to be to sell their house, the one in which they had lived for fifty-five years and in which they had raised their children. Heart wrenching. This was the house they had intended to come out of feet first. Either that or Jim had to come out of retirement and go back into selling real estate, something he patently considered a "younger man's game."

When I arrived at their door, it was clear that Jim TOTALLY thought Feng Shui was complete hooey, thought his wife was out of her mind, and was fully expecting me to walk into his house with black cat in hand and the wizard Merlin's pointed hat planted on my big hair. They had previously planned that during our consultation, Phyllis would take notes and then, once we started walking the different areas of the house, Jim would follow and tape all my suggestions and comments. By the time we reached the Fame area, Jim was nowhere to be found and neither was the tape recorder. It was all too "out there" for him, a Southern good ol' boy who was on the edge of financial ruin and taking advice from someone he considered right below Witch Doctor on the sliding scale of Universal helpers. But Phyllis was one determined dame, and, all beliefs aside, she was willing, at this point, to try anything. I told her about the nine red candles to ignite the Fame energies and how they are especially efficacious when any or all things related to sales are involved (as well as for any enterprise in which you wish to deliver more returns or profit).

About six weeks after our first consult, I was driving a main thoroughfare in my town and happened to notice a FOR SALE sign hanging from a beautiful home on that street. Then I was both shocked and thrilled to see Jim's name hanging from the sign as the point of contact for the sale. "You go, Jim," I prayed.

About six months after that, I was a keynote speaker at a statewide home and garden event when I looked up from my booth and saw the two of them striding toward me with gigantic ear-to-ear grins on their faces. They both looked about twenty years younger than when I had last seen them. Jim informed me that he had indeed gone back into real estate and was in the middle of closing on his sixth home. He even bragged that they could now afford the new driveway that they had been dreaming about putting to the side of their front yard. I looked at Phyllis and acknowledged that her power of intention and all her hard work had paid off, and she said, with a gleam and a twinkle in her eye: "And don't forget the red candles, Ellen. Every morning I hear Jim with that lighter, going click, click, click, click . . . and then whoosh, whoosh, whoosh, as he blows them out. He wouldn't dare begin a day without them!"

If you are looking to heat up your sales activity, your client base, or any aspect of your business or professional opportunities, you should start your day by getting lit . . . with nine red candles, that is.

THE NINE RED CANDLES CURE

Locate the Fame area of your home or office (the far back or center wall) and place nine red candles there. It doesn't matter the size or what color red; choose whatever appeals most to you to achieve the desired effect. Displays of different sizes or even small tea candles can have a huge impact. Whenever there is a time that you want or need to make an indelible impression, light each of these candles individually. You do NOT need to wait for them to burn all the way down. In fact, you need wait only until the wick meets the wax and creates a flame, and then it's time to blow them out . . . unless you want to wait until they burn all the way down. It has been my (and many of my clients') experience that once you get to lighting the ninth candle, you can go back to the first one and begin to blow them out. That was Jim's routine. Mine? Well, let's just say that some days it looks like the inside of St. Patrick's Cathedral around here. But it brings on the heat, and heats up the sales, so, as they say, "If you got 'em, light 'em."

	6	
Wealth and Prosperity	Fame and Reputation	**Relationship, Romance, and Marriage**
Family, Friends, and Ancestors	Health	Children and Creativity
Knowledge and Self-Cultivation	Career	Helpful People and Travel

NOTHING SAYS "I love you" more than, well, "I love you," but knowing exactly how to say this magical phrase in a few very different ways, or even where to say it, can make all the long-lasting, heart-pounding, sweet-dream-inducing difference in the world. The right rear sector of your home, and especially in your bedroom, is the one single space that makes room for two. This Relationship, Romance, and Marriage area also makes sure that every one of your relationships, whether for love or money or any of the other myriad reasons we hook up, are all righted and righteous and full of fuel to go the distance.

As you will soon see, focusing your love-ing intention here helps quite a bit, but not as much as getting rid of all the old stuff still lingering from any of the last breakups. A pair of pink candles placed one alongside the other, pink sheets on the bed, or mating mandarin ducks might help you find "The One," but not until you clear the clutter from under your bed and inside your crammed closet. And, yes, you can tie the two red cords around the back of the bedroom doorknob, or even light the two red lights on either side of the bed, to meet the mate of your soul. But don't expect the perfect someone to appreciate any of these efforts if you don't first appreciate yourself. Or at least not until you make sure your intentions are centered, allowed (read: no going after the married one!), and aligned, and your applications are rigid and routine and last at least the requisite twenty-seven days.

So whether you're looking for love in all the far, back right-hand places or trying to right a relationship gone wrong, or maybe even attempting to win the hearts of your office mates, all the while putting some sizzle back into any partnership, this is the area of intimacy and other not-quite-so-close associations that gets to the heart of every one of these matters. Address this place when you want to encourage happy, healthy, passionate, and prosperous relationships that will nurture, nourish, and nicely partner you up.

The colors associated with romance are reds and pinks, and its place is in the far back right-hand corner of the home, bedroom, or any other place you spend a lot of time. The element here is fire. It shouldn't need to be said that the number associated with this area is 2, does it? Does it really? Okay, just think twice when you're contemplating a few good years of love, laughter, and happily ever after. Just remember, everything here goes better in pairs. Period.

DREAM DATE

How many times have I heard the stories about the well-meaning bubbies (Jewish grandmothers, to the uninitiated) or aunts or sister friends who "know somebody who knows some-body" who is just perfect for you, and will, inevitably, meet and marry you right before you live your oh-so-happily-ever-after life of marital harmony, bliss, and accord? "Just go to sleep," your nana tells you, "and dream of the perfect partner, and then he will magically appear." Whoa there, Grandma. What big dreams YOU have! And this is all supposed to happen without the help of eHarmony or JDate or any of the other three thousand dot-coms that promise the prince or princess without even having to saddle up your horse and leave the comfy "there's no one out there for me, I'm too picky" stable!

But without the hay, get out of the barn and flick the log-on switch. Answer a few relevant questions, and off you go to meet the perfect partner. Here's the scenario I hear the most: So, okay, you went ahead one slightly tipsy night with all your friends egging you on, and you answered a couple of electronic questions, and now there really is someone who wants to meet you for martinis on Friday night. And, shock-a-politan, he sounds really, really great. So now, of course, you are really, really terrified.

Settle down. Soon you will have all the keys to Date Shui to keep this evening engaging all the night long. All you need to do is follow a few (or ALL, if you so choose) of these directions, and you'll never have to don the dating wet suit and go Net surfing again. I promise, these steps are absolutely guaranteed to make sure everything on that special night goes just right.

And speaking of just right, that's exactly where we're starting—in the back right-hand corner of your own bedroom. Let's begin here to enact some simple Shui techniques that will bring the long, the lasting, and the most loving relationship right to your door.

Be COMPLETELY positive that there is not ONE SINGLE THING inside this arena that relates to any long-lost (sorry, sister or mister, read: OVER AND DONE) romance. Lose the old love letters, stuffed animals, and photos taken together at the prom. Replace them with two pink candles in a pair of glass, crystal, or even ceramic holders. From now until you leave for your date (even if that's an imaginary figment in your real-life diary), torch these candles as often as you can, letting them light a spark that will last long after you blow out the flames (because you NEVER leave a candle burning if you're not around . . . right?).

Next, take a good hard look around this whole area and see if any one thing doesn't support this single, soul mate goal. Treadmills and stair steppers taking up space here won't have anyone climbing into your bed anytime soon. Likewise, that pile of laundry—put it away or find another hiding place. Replace it with a sexy little bit of boxer or red, strappy teddy, perhaps, to add to the heat and the action as much as the candles can.

Such little wisps of lingerie or alluring undies only begin to energetically tie the two of you together. You need to be sure to have something on hand that stimulates ALL five of the senses. Remember that anything that attracts ANY of the senses also attracts strong and supportive energies, or Chi, so drip a couple of drops of the sexy-smelling ylang-ylang essential oil onto any low-wattage lightbulb and take serious steps to stimulate a scentual romance. Make music for and with the two of you. Take it from me, prepare and make it easy to access, soothing and sexy. These songs should make your heart sing. You already have the two candles, but to add some massage oils nearby, some red sheets (you can even put one red satin sheet between the mattress and the box spring if you don't want to appear too, too aggressive), will show a smidge of inventiveness with a whole lotta love (and Shui) attached. Last, something sweet to eat close by, a chocolate Kiss or two, will seal the deal and have everyone licking their lips.

Just in case, there are rules for the restaurant, too. Here are some simple Shui suggestions that will make this date the one you will be telling your children when they want all the details about the first night the two of you met. Kidsmet.

As you arrive at Château Le Shui, allow the guy to be the one who handles communication between the two of you and the hostess or maître d'. This applies even if the Miss is the first through the door (and she should be!).

To continue to put yourselves in a position of the greatest advantage for the most romantically wonderful outcome, tradition says to be sure, as you are both seated, that Mister gets the chair that faces the front or the entrance to the eatery. It's even better if he can also have his back against a wall (seriously, NO pun intended). This gives him what is commonly called "the command position," where he will then feel courageous, confident, and completely sure of himself . . . and of his date, too! This makes for a quite comforting first, fourth, or fifteenth date. Believe me.

And, as antiquated as this might sound, let him pay. You'll both get a jolt out of that. Unless, as is sometimes the situation, you have agreed to a different arrangement beforehand. Remember, there's an inherent electricity from the energetic perspective if he handles the bill and assumes the charge, so let him pay and enjoy it!

From my experience, if you follow these tips and techniques and feel good about your choices and decisions, and if you truly deep down inside believe that this advice can help you find "The One," then it will. Somewhere down the line, when you are recounting this story to family and friends, you can remind them how just by moving that StairMaster out of that one essential romance and relationship area, you moved one step closer to the love of your life, the step that preceded your slow, beautiful stride down the aisle together.

VALENTINE'S DAY SHUI

It's pretty predictable that every year, right after New Year's, my phone will start ringing off the hook with clients wondering just exactly how they can get hooked . . . up, that is. People from New York to California and everywhere in between have just made it through the holidays and begun their New Year—with either a bang or a bust—and they are beginning to think about V-Day. Why is this holiday so hampered by relationship worries? As my client Tory put it, "I just hate the fact that I even have to think about it at all. But I just got through New Year's and I

Attract That Special Someone

Two Proven Powerful Cures:

When you are really ready to stop the search and get real for real, two ancient advisos have been passed down to me orally that are said to lead to the light at the end of this tunnel of love. I've seen both cures bring big and beneficial results, and I look forward to you not only attracting the special someone but also learning that he or she is the soul mate you have been searching for. Always be clear, concise, and careful about what you ask for. The "guy in the big house" might just be shooting you e-mails from Alcatraz.

• Leave a small hand-held mirror outside, reflective side facing up, on any three nights of any full moon to "charge" the mirror. At the end of this three-day interval, move the mirror indoors but cover it immediately with a piece of silk or satin. BE PERFECTLY SURE that no one else can either see or, HEAVEN forbid, touch it. Then put it somewhere safe for the next twenty-seven days. Mark your calendar. On the twenty-seventh day, you should orchestrate being in the presence of the potential soul mate and having access to your other mate, the magic mirror. When that person is not paying attention, flash the mirror in their direction, so you can capture their "essence" (okay, this means, as much as possible, their face) in it. Be careful that the object of your affection doesn't see you reflecting your own intentions. Once you have successfully snapped up these energies, put the mirror back in its case and place it where you were keeping it before. Now that you have elicited the energies of your intended and are holding them in your heart and in some other special place, you simply will not believe how quickly that person will be looking at you in a whole different light. More than one of you will now be moonstruck!

- Here's another surefire cure to capture the heart of your amour. Take two smiling photos—one of happy you alone and one of your amour smiling, alone—and place them face-to-face. Then wrap this little love package ninety-nine times with red ribbon, string, thread, or yarn. Place the pictures in the Romance/Relationship area (back right-hand corner of the main floor of your house or bedroom) and place a pair of wooden chopsticks atop the photos. The chopsticks should be tied together with nine inches of red ribbon, thread, or string so that they form an X before you place them on top of the picture pair of you. This should be left alone for twenty-seven days, and at the end of that juncture you will take the two pictures, still tied together, and throw them into any moving source of water that you reside near—a stream, a river, a pond, a lake, or an ocean. The organic-water part is important; therefore, you can't use the kitchen sink or any source inside the home to float these lovebirds away. So, though this cure may take you outside your apartment or house for a brisk walk, it's well worth this effective effort. Go ahead and put the chopsticks away; you can use them once you are married and want to have kids. They will also come in handy on the Feng Shui fertility front, like white on rice.

didn't have a date then either. I just don't want to be alone for Valentine's Day, too!"

Tory is not alone, at least not in those sorts of sentiments anyway. Last year, another client, Linda, a sixty-something woman from Atlanta, called, asking me to help her "navigate Valentine's

Day," as she phrased it. Linda explained that no matter how much plastic surgery she has done to her body or even how much more plastic she has in her Louis Vuitton wallet, she still hasn't met the right guy. I asked her a few questions and realized that though she constantly said she wanted to meet (and marry) her soul mate, she hadn't really opened herself fully to what a true and realistic romantic relationship would require. In other words, she'd adjusted her face by lifting her brows while also slurping some fat out of a thigh or two, too, but, after a series of not too satisfying "encounters" with men that just "didn't click," she had just about given up on the prospect of hooking up with the man of her dreams.

It was clear that it was time for Linda to start living and loving Linda before she could find the right mate to do that exact same thing. I suggested that she might want to begin that process by taking herself out on what she called the "perfect" date for her. "Just enjoy being with your own company and treat yourself the way you want to be treated by a potential partner"—that was my advice. This little Shui cure will encourage a BIG response from Universal energies when the search for the perfect partner has begun in earnest. Search for and then marry your own self first.

Another woman I know was in a very different but curiously similar predicament. Frances and I had met at one of my seminars, when she approached me to ask more about how Feng Shui might help her find someone to share her life with. As I listened to her, she told me that she had recently ended a rather abusive relationship. She told me that although she wanted to find another true love, she felt bruised and fearful of being "out there" again. We set up a consultation at her house.

As soon as I stepped over her threshold, I was surprised by the sheer number of paintings, sculpture, and other pieces of art that occupied so much space in her home. It wasn't the amount of art that rattled me, though, but rather the singular theme: All of the art in some way or another depicted a single African-American female, which she was. And while on the one hand I could sense that Frances felt she needed the power and protection these female icons provided, on the other it was immediately clear that these symbols were also blocking the entry of any significant male energy into her life.

All of these women—Tory, Linda, and Frances—contacted me in the month before Valentine's Day. I offered them similar cures (see below) for very different reasons as well as for their own singular situations. The results? Tory became proactive and asked out a guy whom she had met at the New Year's Eve party (the one she didn't have a date to), and they arranged to meet for a Valentine's Day lunch. They remain good friends to this day, but she's still looking. Linda organized a V-Day dinner with some of her best friends at a swell dinner club and met a lovely man seated at the table to her right. They've now been seeing each other for nine months. And Frances balanced her belongings by bringing in some strong male energy to complement the comforting female Chi all over her house. On a pilgrimage to a local bookstore one day, she met a tall, handsome black man while they were both browsing for books about Feng Shui! After a brief chat, the man asked her out for coffee, and a year and a half later they married. I am not making this up!

Valentine's Day relies on the energies associated with the Romance/Love sector of the Feng Shui Bagua. Here are some keys to unlock some hearts:

- One of the best ways to activate your relationship energies is by clearing out clutter in your Relationship and Romance sector (back right-hand corner of either the main floor of your home or, equally as potent in this case, your BED-

ROOM!). Now is the time to assess this sector, and if you find you've kept anything here that reminds you of an old flame (love letters, pictures of the two of you together, or the stuffie he won at the state fair), that's exactly where these things should go . . . up in flames. I'm soooo not kidding. Toss them, give them away, or even bury them in the backyard, but GET THEM OUT OF YOUR RELATIONSHIP AREA! You need to clear the area, both physically and mentally, for a new relationship to take its place.

• Once the old is out of the way, you can get ready to welcome the new. According to Feng Shui, pink is the main color and 2 is the number associated with Romance, so keep this in mind when you place two of anything in this sector of your bedroom, or in the Relationship area of your home. Again, a good way to start is by putting two ceramic candlesticks with two pink candles in your Relationship and Romance sector and lighting them as often as you wish. Especially when you're looking for that hot date. Sort of a Feng Shui match.com.

• If the candles don't strike your fancy, then it is fine to place two other objects here. Traditional Feng Shui says to put a pair of lovebirds or wooden ducks in this area, but you can choose two of anything that represents something you enjoy doing with the person you have in mind. The pair symbolizes your intended partnership. Two snowboards, two toy NASCARs, two disposable cameras . . . get the picture?

• Now, here is my pièce de résistance—the power of the following cure is not to be underestimated, and it is virtually guaranteed to work. But pay attention: It requires a lot of focus and follow-through, so it's not for the faint of heart or the uncommitted. But, if you're serious about giving your heart to someone who wants to be equally committed, then do the following: Turn on a light in the Relationship area of your bedroom for three hours a day for forty-nine consecutive days. If you skip a day, you have to start all over again. Any three hours of every day will do, but be sure if you are traveling during this forty-nine-day period that you either leave that love light burning or have that same person who comes to feed the fish feed your heart's desires and turn the light on and off. Or just use timers.

• Another powerful cure is enacted by placing a picture of either the Mystic Knot or the Double Happiness Symbol in the Relationship sector of your house or bedroom. This will assist you in attracting the love of your life. These Feng Shui symbols of undying love and affection promise long and healthy relationships free from separation, suffering, or heartbreak. These are two of the LUCKIEST of love symbols. Once you've found your love, then you can move these symbols closer to your bed to maintain the magic.

Happy Valentine's Day!

STORIES TO (GET AND) KEEP YOU ENGAGED

Several years ago I first encountered "Maya," a local newscaster who wanted to do an on-air story with me about a house on which I was consulting and helping to design and build for a local parade-of-homes pageant. During the course of our meetings and getting to know each other, I realized that Maya was

Searching for Your Soul Mate

Are you single and looking for the person who will be walking alongside you for the rest of your days? The one who will be holding your hand and giving you that same tingly feeling that Mark Mapother did the first time he sneaked a kiss in the back of the bleachers during the seventh grade football play-offs? Well, if you are really and truly serious and no longer interested in playing the field, try this next secret, secret, secret Shui cure to kick off your efforts and land your one true love.

According to this ancient custom, a single woman hoping to mate for life should wear a ring on the forefinger of her right hand. The ring can be jade or amethyst or even rose quartz (or any other gemstone that you love), but it needs to stay put on that index finger for three solid months to make sure you are pointed in the right direction. If you remove the ring for any great length of time (longer than to lather up or stuff the turkey), then you need to cleanse it by leaving it out in the sunlight for seven days; you can do this easily by putting it on a windowsill. Then start the three-month affair all over again.

Legend holds that once you meet the man of your dreams, and you are absolutely POSITIVE that you want to marry him, you should move that ring to the middle finger of the right hand and leave it there another three months.

Once you have walked into the proverbial sunset together, you will finally move that ring to your right-hand ring finger, where it will stay with you through your happily ever after. (To answer a question I always get asked, "What sort of ring can move from finger to finger without having to be sized?" Well, you have two choices: Line your ring with an elastic inner cording, or have your ring sized—while you're sizing up your potential mate, you can be doing the same thing with this ring! Both of them clearly need your time and your consideration.)

quickly coming to see the validity of using Feng Shui as a viable method of constructing a better reality. She was really getting that these techniques can be employed not only on the traditional footprint and floor plan of any building but also as a blueprint for the whole of one's life. However, because of the way in which our friendship was developing, she preferred that her curiosity be kept out of the professional "conflict of interest" column as well as that other one that killed the proverbial cat. Maya wanted to keep her paws clean but did want to hear any tips that could help her claw her way to the top anchor spot in her newsroom sandbox.

So we began a little consulting that we kept our little secret, and soon her career was purring away; in fact, I used to call her my "in the Feng Shui closet" client. Until, of course, after assessing both her home and her office and after creating needed adjustments in both, she quickly rose through the ranks from street reporter to the coveted five o'clock news coanchor, making her both believer and beholder in one swift move up the local studio stairs.

At the same time she was also heavily invested in a relationship with a guy who was abusive, alcoholic, and emotionally stunted. Okay, after scampering with such success in such a quick amount of time in her professional efforts, it was no surprise that she wanted to know if Feng Shui could prod this man to propose. There is indeed a "secret" Feng Shui cure to get engaged, and it involves using boulders, or relationship building blocks, along with your intentions. But because I thought this guy was such a loser, I was really hesitant to share this information with her so that she might then go and share her life with him. I was stuck between a rock and a hard spot. More on Maya in a minute. Let me share another quick love story.

Sonny, on the other hand, really loved his gal, and she, apparently (and according to him since she and I had never met), really loved him but was truly afraid of commitment. She had been through two nasty relationships that had resulted in two bitter divorces and was content just living with Sonny. But he wanted the marriage, the house, the kids, the white picket fence—the whole thing. And he wanted his girlfriend to want it just as badly as he did.

In both of these cases—Sonny with his beloved girlfriend, and Maya, the newscaster—I ended up offering the same information and then stepped aside to let the rocks fall where they may (but, hopefully, that was close enough to where I told them to put them).

For Sonny, he and his girlfriend got married nine months exactly to the day that he performed the cure, and they are now living with their blended family behind a white picket fence about three miles from me. And Maya is living kind of close, too . . . but not with the loser. She met and married a Greek shipping magnate who treats her like gold and plies her with the same. And oompah! They are now expecting their first son!

Drumroll, please. Here is the Engagement Cure:

- Place eight boulders (you can also use stones or river rocks, but tradition dictates that I say "boulders") in a circular arrangement preferably outside in your Relationship area (back left-hand corner of your property) or inside in the same space of your main floor. You may pile the stones in a pyramidal shape, but it must remain circular (think: wedding ring!).

- Spray-paint one rock or stone gold and position it in the center or atop all the others.

- Then, in some derivation of that magical number 9 (nine inches, eighteen inches—whatever fits your boulders or rocks), tie as many inches of red ribbon, string, thread, or yarn around that top rock, the one that is painted gold. Leave this configuration in place for at least nine months, and don't forget that these energies will be working to engage all the marriage energies they can muster.

· Once you are sufficiently tied to each other, dismantle your personal Stonehenge and move on to building your own wonderful life together.

WEDDING DAY SHUI

We all dream of our wedding day, and that dream is always perfect. A wedding represents the beginning of two lives being enjoined. It is a gathering of friends and family to witness this union. It's an opportunity to wish the new couple well. And it's a day that evokes our highest hopes. Which is why wedding planners comprise a $50-million-a-year industry! Luckily, they felt the same way about weddings five thousand years ago. Feng Shui offers successful secrets and ancient cures that even today ensure that your day of bridal bliss will be one marked by the Three Great Blessings—Health, Happiness, and Prosperity.

So whether you're planning a low-key wedding in your backyard or an extravaganza, here are some hot tips for the coolest couples:

· When choosing your gown, opt for a shade that's slightly off-white, such as beige, ivory, candlelight, or gold. The same rule applies to guys (dress shirts, vests, and bow ties). Your fabric choices are also important and should combine heavy and light fabrics to add balance and good energy—this rule applies not only to the bride but also to the groom and the wedding party. Heavily textured fabrics, such as brocade, satin, and shantung, carry quiet energy—considered yin, or receptive. Light fabrics, such as organza, tulle, and chiffon, are louder and more excitable materials—those are yang, or considered more aggressive.

- Proper lighting at your ceremony and reception is very important to pave the way for a bright future. Make sure that both your ceremony and your reception sites have windows that offer plenty of natural light. Try to avoid too much overhead lighting, as this can create shadow. Use elegant side lighting in its place.

- The color scheme you choose for your wedding will set the mood and reflect you as a couple. Consider the meanings of these wedding day colors:

  Red: Not only is it a traditional Chinese wedding color, accenting your wedding day with red also creates a strong atmosphere of love and romance.

  Pink: Perfect for a younger couple, pink evokes a sense of fun, playfulness, and lightheartedness.

  Purple and violet: Good for a smaller, more intimate wedding celebration with close family and friends, purples give off a very sexy, passionate vibe.

  Black and white: A favorite combination for creating positive Shui, black and white together represent a strong, balanced relationship—as in the well-known yin-and-yang symbol.

  Blues and greens: A good color combo for a couple who have known each other for many years, or even for a second wedding, because blues and greens promote a calm and secure quality and feeling.

Yellow: This bright, sunny color is the hue of cheerfulness and the perfect color to add to a less-than-well-lit ceremony or reception space.

• Also, on that special wedding day, it is considered great and lasting good luck to release white doves (or any other bird that is indigenous to your locale) from "captivity." The dove always symbolizes peace and patience, love and understanding, and is said to bless the union with all of those very same qualities. It is also thought that this gesture will guarantee a life of "many freedoms" for both bride and groom, as it will give both mates "wings to fly."

• Brides "in the know" sometimes place a mirror inside the church or other ceremony location to ward off evil influences as the marriage takes place. Some brides even position a mirror on themselves to keep away malevolent spirits or energies.

• One of my favorite tips to assure a long and happy marriage comes from an ancient Eastern axiom that says "A daughter who marries is like spilled water—she cannot look back." This saying has generated a brand-new tradition to help keep any marriage beautiful and blessed. As the couple leaves the reception, the bride and groom should each spill a cup of water on the road behind them. They should drive off without ever looking back. It is said that to do this will forever fortify a marriage with few or no regrets.

SHORT AND SWEET, THE HONEYMOON

The actual term *honeymoon* is derived from the magical custom that says if a newly wedded couple were to hole up somewhere and drink a honey-infused wine for the first thirty days of their married life, then every other day of their marriage will be filled with sweetness, shared love, and fertility. In fact, honey imbibed in any brew or concoction at the wedding ceremony itself is believed to honor and enact two tremendous traditions or gifts that every bride and groom should have listed on their registry— purity and wisdom for their long and happy life.

The first gift honey delivers comes from it being so organic and virtually untouched by human hand (unless it's the giant one with the big canvas glove on it), and the buzz is that the purity in the honey will always and forever protect the couple from anything untoward or evil.

Honey has also long been held as a symbol or representative of the combination of newly acquired love mixed with a big dose of wisdom; again, these gifts should always be at the top of the dowry or registry list, even in front of the china and crystal.

So if Cupid has readied, aimed, fired, and flown, then you might just want to aid any aphrodisiac efforts with a little concoction of your own:

Warm a cup of honey in a bain-marie, or Dutch oven, and add to it about a half to one cup of dried or even fresh lavender blossoms. As the honey starts to bubble up, immediately remove it from the heat. Let this mixture sit for at least thirty to forty minutes and then strain out the lavender. Use this lavender honey as a warm massage oil, or add it to your evening wine or tea. It has even been known to work well as a lubricant. Either way, it'll make for a memorable (and tasty) honeymoon night!

BREAKUP OR DIVORCE

Chi happens. It's happening all around us all the time, whether we can actually see it or not. That is the nature of energy, energy that is constantly circulating all around us at every moment of every second of every day. It's always moving, always and eternally in motion, because, well, if it weren't, then time would stand still and the Universe would simply implode. And, sometimes, that's exactly what we perceive to be happening on our personal planets when a change occurs that challenges us or makes us question our very selves and our souls, our decisions and our debacles, like, for instance, during an ugly divorce or a really gut-wrenching breakup.

But if we could only keep in mind that as we change and grow, sometimes our relationships can't keep the pace, and then remember that's the very nature of change and it's OKAY. If we were all able to remember this truth, then maybe we could all be

Coming Home from the Honeymoon

There is an ancient custom of carrying the bride over the threshold, which stems from the idea that putting down a runway carpet or strewing it with floral petals will keep a newly married couple from any evil that might be lurking just below the surface. It's even better when the groom carries the bride into their new lair of love; doing this, he provides yet an additional layer of protection from those nasty little annoying love monsters.

Remember, it is also considered very fortunate for the bride to enter her home with her beloved by her side (or in his arms) by way of the main entry ONLY, and she should be exceedingly careful never to trip or fall. (She should beg the groom to get buff before the big day so he can do a little light lifting for Luck's sake!)

Bloom and Grow Forever

Keep your love fresh and alive every year by planning the perfect wedding anniversary gift. Not only are fresh flowers a simple yet extraordinary way of keeping your marriage Chi at it's optimum best, but they will always leave a lingering layer of love long after those roots have hit the road. One powerful way to pave the way to a long-lasting and adoring love life is to gift your spouse with a replica of your wedding bouquet every year on your anniversary. A romantic bouquet that renews the energies of your vows will WOW WOW WOW! Of course, we are talking replica here, so the extravagance that was possibly involved in paying for that first bunch of love need not necessarily be replicated as well. But I can just hear Whitney now in the background singing, "And I (iiiiiiii) will always love you!" Say exactly that with these flowers.

just a bit gentler with ourselves and also with our fragile (and maybe even heartbroken?) psyches. Is it better to stay stuck and stale and unhappy than to move on to other life-enhancing possibilities? And yet I see and, mostly, hear it all the time—the C word. No, not cancer. Or even that other horrible one, clutter. No, what I hear when divorce or a breakup is involved is the word I truly despise the most: *can't*.

"I can't because" . . . "the kids," "the length of time we've been together," "his health," "the dog"—pick one or pick all, it's all the same, just an excuse not to move on. Here are some more "I can't move on" excuses: "There's not enough money to pay for two places"; "Her mother lives with us"; "I'm in love with someone else and it'll kill him/her"; "I'm pregnant"; "He's sterile"; and the list just goes on and on and on. And no one gets anywhere except more and more frightened, unhappy, and resentful. And then someone will, I promise, because this is yet another Universal Law, get sick and find some other way to leave the relationship rather than via the traditional route through the court system. Unless this road is the one consciously chosen to travel, you can expect a whole lot more detours, disease, and toxicity to follow you.

I absolutely understand that at one time even the most doomed of relationships began on an optimistic note and maybe even in a place of peace and hope and, yes, even BIG Love, the kind with the capital L. But somewhere between the starter house and the last Fourth of July backyard barbecue, rancor, rage, and bitterness have moved in as well, and now it's time to shut the gas grill, stop the emotional fireworks, and move on. Fueling any other sort of future will only erode any potential you have for having a wonderful rest of your life.

In an ideal world, there should be no blame or shame or guilt about splitting up the towels, the CDs, and the blankets. There should only be joy that you came together to learn lessons from each other, and that you've decided for the good of all involved that you will take those lessons with you when you go your separate ways. You were LUCKY to learn those lessons from a partner, and now you have them FOREVER in your heart and in your head and in your soul as you go forward in your life. And, hopefully, the next time around you'll know more of who you are and why you've ended up here, rebuilding your own personal planet, this time exactly how you WANT it to be! As you are being the architect of your future, you will enjoy your genius and beauty as well.

As in so many cases that I witness and observe, if you "can't" see your way to forgiveness or happiness over this breakup and/ or separation and/or divorce at this moment in time, I completely understand. I have MANY clients who prefer instead to spend their days planning for the time when they have their Rolls-Royce, have lost those thirty pounds, and have someone twenty years younger hanging on their arm and on their every word. And who do they happen to run into at the local bistro— their ex. For now, whatever gets you through the split is okay with me, as long as you still use the following advice, because these tips, when utilized with proper intent and a good (albeit broken) heart can even help to manifest that last fantasy.

Let's plant you firmly in your fabulous future and help that garden grow:

- No matter the circumstances, you should always at least change the mattress of the bed you shared. It's unreasonable (with the price of a brand-new bed) to believe that everyone who is breaking up (from college sweethearts just starting out to couples who barely can make ends meet) is able to buy a new bed. So instead, opt for a new mattress, or, at the very least, "cleanse" the one you shared with your partner (with sage or salt) and get a new set of sheets to welcome your new set of dreams.

- If you do replace your linens, soft pinks and greens help to heal a broken heart. Period.

- Try to put a fresh coat of paint on the bedroom walls. And, if at all possible, rearrange the furniture. There's an old adage in Feng Shui that says moving twenty-seven things in your bedroom or in your house as a whole will bring in a whole new world of energies, and what better time than now to test that theory? At the very least, move your bed, vacuum under and around it, and then put it back but not exactly where it was. Move it a few inches. (If you are ready and looking for a new partner, women should paint their bedroom walls a pale shade of peach or pink. Men, you're on your own, but I do know you are supposed to hang a picture of cherry blossoms to bring a great girl into your life.)

• For at least three months after the split, try to keep fresh flowers in your bedroom. But get rid of them AS SOON AS they begin to wilt. And get rid of all the dried ones ALL OVER the house.

• For the first twenty-seven days after the split, open your windows, WIDE, every day, if even for a few seconds, to get a fresh perspective, to clean out the old and bring in the new, and to take a break and catch your breath.

• When you are ready, do a MAJOR cleanse of YOUR things. Get rid of anything that no longer serves or speaks to your strengths, hopes, and dreams. If you don't love it, need it, or use it, let it go. That will be your motto moving forward. (And while you're at it, do you still need ANY of the wedding trousseaus? Just asking. Because I already know that answer, and so do YOU.)

• Keep a minimum of two pillows on your bed and try to keep things in your bedroom in pairs. Even if you are not ready for a new partner, this will help you keep good company while you are finding your way through this patch. Besides, pillows should always be kept in multiples of two, so no harm, no foul.

• If you must wallow, go ahead. But please, at least glance at a calendar and give yourself a date when you will know you have moved from a place of self-pity to the one called "personal empowerment." Play the music you both loved and lived with, but keep an ear cocked for smoother harmonies in your future and start dancing to those while you are running the bathwater and pouring ten drops of honeysuckle flower essence into it. You can purchase this at any health-food store. Put four drops under your tongue or put ten into a bath; either way, I have clients who SWEAR (LOUDLY) that this single "tip" made their breakup the easiest thing they ever did!

- Speaking of music, play soft, calming, and soothing sounds during the day while you are out of the house (or even in it). On so many different levels this will cleanse and clear negativity while promoting peace and harmony for you to return to.

I Do, I Did, and Now I Just Don't Know

Maybe the marriage isn't completely over but is merely going through a rough and rocky patch, or what I like to call a "growth spurt." IF that's the case, you can try to revive the original intent of your relationship by seeing this through all the way to the very last vow. Here are some ways from traditions that have stood the test of time to help you trek that terrain:

- First, tie nine inches of red ribbon, string, thread, or yarn to an amethyst crystal and tie the crystal to the foot of the side of the bed your partner sleeps on. This will ground their energy inside that special room and firmly plant their Chi next to yours.

- Watch your words! If you are constantly telling others what a mess your marriage is, guess what? You will have sounded the death knell like the town crier with no one else to blame but yourself! Even while going through the same shaky ground that EVERY relationship goes through, reaffirm that you will come out of this on the other side all the better for the test. "I love everyone and everyone loves me" is an effective affirmation that literally will come true. And one of those people who really and truly love you can now become your cherished partner.

- Take a yard of red ribbon (or string, thread, or yarn) and cut it into four nine-inch "ties." Hang one in each of these four energy areas: Helpful People (bottom, or lower, left-hand corner of the home), Career (center, or bottom middle of the tic-tac-toe board created on the footprint of your main floor as you stand at your front door), Family/Friends (center of the left-hand wall of the main floor), and Wealth (far back left-hand corner of the main floor). Hang each one of them high, and let them call back romance and relatively normal relations into what might have become a somewhat rocky path or partnership. This is another one of those cures that call upon some cosmic therapy. My experience is that if BOTH of you really want to preserve the partnership, this adjustment is as effective as the two-hundred-dollar-an-hour marriage counselor.

I Do, I Did, and Now I Don't, or The Dirty Divorce

If you and your partner are indeed splitting, and your split has become particularly contentious, there are a couple of ways to point your ex out the door and then freeze him or her out of your life:

• Take any picture of your ex, with ONLY him or her in the photo, and place it underneath a cactus plant that is in a red container (terra-cotta, red ceramic, red plastic cup, whatever). Place the picture under the cactus in the Fame area in the house (far back center, or middle space on the main floor) and leave it there for twenty-seven days. As we all know, the cactus plant (even a Christmas cactus) is flora non grata in the world of Feng Shui because of its propensity to point Sha, or bad, Chi at us from all its little stabbing thorns. But in this case, the cactus is used for exactly that same purpose—to point this person out of our lives, hopefully with a whole lot less stabbing and a whole lot more ease and grace. At the end of the twenty-seven days, move the cactus outdoors (planted outside your home, the cactus actually protects your space) and burn the photo. This cure actually works well with anyone who needs to be gone from your life. As does the next one.

- In red, write the name of your ex and put that paper into an ice cube tray in your freezer. If that's not possible, then simply write down his or her name, put it in a plastic bag with water, and place it somewhere in the back of the freezer. The implications here are pretty obvious, but just in case: You are attempting to freeze this person out of your affairs and out of your life. Don't be too surprised, though, when the next time you run into this person you're met with some pretty icy-cold stares. That's the point, isn't it? By the way, this piece of advice is a secret Shui that has been known to be used successfully in almost every single tradition that I have studied, even the ones that didn't have stainless seven-footers, or even a forty-two-inch Viking side-by-side.

7		
Wealth and Prosperity	Fame and Reputation	Relationship, Romance, and Marriage
Family, Friends, and Ancestors	Health	**Children and Creativity**
Knowledge and Self-Cultivation	Career	Helpful People and Travel

AS ART LINKLETTER has so adeptly observed, "Kids say [and DO!] the darndest things." But darn if there isn't a place inside everyone's living spaces to make sure that those very same things are supportive and motivating, helping our next generations to bring fairy-tale endings to all that they begin, all the way around—with appropriate intention and transformational actions leading the way, of course!

The ability to transform intention into matter creatively is the energy of the Feng Shui Children and Creativity sector. This space is always located in the middle of the right-hand wall of the main floor of the home. Equally powerful, though, is this same area located in the center of the right-hand wall of any child's bedroom (standing at the door to their sleeping space, make the room as close to a square or rectangle as you can and then find the middle of the right-hand wall, and, there, you have it).

Whether giving birth to a baby, pushing out a creative endeavor, or acknowledging your own "inner child," this is the space to take a long, hard look at. Making adjustments to the energies associated with the Children/Creativity arena replenishes the playful wellspring within. The element accorded to these energies is METAL, so sometimes just adding a bit of the same to that space allows all to mine and then manifest childlike joy, belief, expression, and ingenuity. Therefore, an accepted and encouraged adjustment to make inside this area is to place seven metal coins here (seven also being a number affiliated with the Chi of Children and the energies associated with your Creativity). This arena will then activate or trigger childlike balance and bliss—for the kid in all of us.

The color ascribed to Children and Creativity is white and/or any color from the pastel palette. So placing a white flowering plant into this *gua* will promote great growth experiences while leaving no leaf unturned in your efforts to bring childhood and all its challenges the best and happiest endings. The cures that follow ascribed to this arena come from ancient customs, traditions, and some tried-and-true methods from the world of Feng Shui.

Briefly, all actions and intentions accorded to this Children and (your) Creativity sector will benefit from your determination and efforts. And, well, darn if they don't just make you feel like a kid again, too. Our blockbuster journey of a thousand miles will now begin with some baby steps (literally!). Enjoy the walkabout.

I'M (FINALLY!!!) PREGNANT!

Infertility. Been there, done that. And I've done that and that and, yeah, even that, too. All in my copious and exhaustive efforts to have a child. I always think of Marisa Tomei in her Academy Award–winning performance in the hilarious film *My Cousin Vinny* when she stands in front of her on-screen lover, played by Joe Pesci, stomping her stiletto and imitating her maternal clock ticking while her childbearing years tock away. My own timekeeper, like a monthly Big Ben, tolling in my head while breaking my hopeful heart, always reminded me that I was still kidless in Miami.

There they were, hundreds of books and thousands of well-wishers all telling me how to get pregnant. I still even remember the woman who lived in my condo and kept reminding me, every single time I saw her, that the odds were waaaay against me. "It's actually easier to catch a fish," she would say as the elevator took another three thousand years to hit the lobby, "than it is to get pregnant."

I wanted to ask her, every single time, (A) how she knew this ridiculous yet seemingly unerringly accurate fact, and (B) how she thought that reminding me of this every time we breathed the same air might, in ANY remote way, actually help me in my unstoppable efforts at childbearing.

I am not a doctor nor am I a fertility specialist, although, after everything I've gone through, I sometimes think myself qualified to be called both. But there is something that I AM called now and that's "Mom." Not only did I finally find some Feng Shui keys that helped me to unlock my own inability to conceive and carry a beautiful child through to birth, but I have also seen this information work wonders for an impressive list of clients who have come to me with these same hopes, wishes, and bouncing-baby dreams.

I absolutely understand and acknowledge that advances made in modern-day allopathic medicine helped me immeasurably on this quest. But I also truly believe, down to my bones, that it was three specific Feng Shui cures that eventually enabled me to get pregnant, stay pregnant, and deliver the delight of my life eleven short years ago.

But don't take my word for it. Consider these two stories from the client files, and then, if you, too, are trying to get pregnant, try the Baby Shui cures (listed below), and when you're sending baby announcements, please don't forget me. Who knows, your own story might just make my next book. After, of course, you've rested up from your easy and grace-filled birth (and the billion sleepless nights that follow!).

My most famous fertility story is Jen's because it made it on the air! I had been doing some business with a retail-marketing exec who was helping me to bring my small Feng Shui–related product line to the store shelves in giant Nordstrom. The woman who was helping me hone my pitch had a secretary whom I seemed to speak to more than the actual exec herself. One day, the secretary shared with me that although she didn't really believe in Feng Shui, she had been single a long time and was really hoping to find a relationship. She asked if I would come to her house for a consult and to see if we could find her Mr. Right. But since encountering me was the first time she'd ever even heard of Feng Shui, she invited her daughter, Jennifer (someone more Shui savvy), to sit in on the appointment for moral support.

As it happened, Jennifer, a locally well-known and beloved radio personality, had been suffering the trials of infertility herself and been none too shy about sharing her stories on the air. After we finished assessing her mom's space, Jennifer then confided in me that she and her husband had been trying "for years" to get pregnant with no "luck" (no pun!). According to her doctors there wasn't any cause or reason (the amorphous "gray" area of infertility that I, too, knew all too well), but, well, something just wasn't working with one of them as they battled on from one specialist to another.

I told her about my own experiences and she eagerly agreed that she would try the three powerful adjustments that have been working since Feng Shui started to be recorded in the East some six thousand years ago. About six months later, I answered my office phone only to be told that I was "Live . . . on the air." It was Jennifer hosting her radio show, and, she said, besides telling her husband and her loved ones, she wanted me (and her however many listeners!) to be "the first to know" that she was four months' pregnant. Then she gave all the success props to the Feng Shui cures they utilized.

Jennifer is off the air now because, I'm pretty sure, she just had either baby number two or baby number three!

Marianne was forty-one when she decided she wanted to become pregnant again. She already had a two-year-old daughter, Faith, but wanted to try one last time "to give Faith a baby brother or sister." After about ten months of trying the "old-fashioned way" and because of her age, Marianne's ob-gyn suggested she consult with a fertility specialist. She chose a doctor at one of the most prestigious university hospitals in the country (considerably well respected, in fact, for the success rate of their infertility program). After the standard battery of blood work and tests, the results were in and they weren't what she wanted to hear. According to these standards, Marianne had "less than a 5 percent chance" at conception and carrying through to live birth. Because her eggs were "old and tired and too few in number," her specialist wouldn't even consider the myriad possible invasive methods now available to almost anyone with a deep desire and even deeper pockets.

Marianne went home and cried for three days. Then she dried her eyes and whetted her appetite for "other, more alternative" ways of getting pregnant. And that's exactly where I came in. She had heard of the success that some of my clients were having conceiving and she wanted in.

I told her matter-of-factly what you are about to read here. And the last time I tried to tell her anything, I told her to put her questions in an e-mail and send them to me. I couldn't hear her because of the babies (twins!) crying in the background—the pitfalls sometimes associated with my job. But I can take it, really I can.

FERTILITY SHUI

- Place a pair of wooden elephants on either side of your bedroom door or one wooden elephant with a stone on his back at your front door. The stone should be one that you have picked up from outside and preferably sits easily atop the elephant so that you're not placing it back up there every time the door opens. (What you place on the back of the "wish-granting" elephant can result in different things, according to Feng Shui; one carrying a crystal can call in movement in your Career energies while one with coins carries Wealth to you!) An elephant with a rock on its back beckons children. It is also widely noted from fertility traditions across the board that you can rub the elephant's forehead for a little added Fortune as you tread the fertility trail.

• Sleep on green sheets. I know couples who were so skeptical about using these age-old techniques that this one was the ONLY adjustment they were willing to make. I'm god-mother to one of their kids now. This works, well, like a charm.

• Take a pair of chopsticks and tie them crosswise (so that they form an X), together with either nine or eighteen inches of red ribbon, string, or yarn. Place them in the Children/Creativity area of your home or in this same space in the room you sleep in (the middle of the right-hand wall of the main floor or the bedroom were it to be laid out as a tic-tac-toe board). Leave them there for at least twenty-seven days, or go for the gusto and leave them there for what a normal gestational period of your pregnancy would be . . . nine months.

• Paint one wall of your bedroom a light shade of yellow. It is preferred that the wall painted is the one that rests solidly behind the headboard of your bed. Yellow is said to aid all efforts at conception. No worries, though, if you can't change the color of a wall—just use one (or more) of these other fertility suggestions, and you'll be toting a diaper bag in no time at all.

• Place anything "childlike" (stuffed animals, pictures of children playing, crayons, etc.) in the Children area of your bedroom. Feng Shui traditionally uses a stuffed tiger here (although the tiger is considered to be the protector of this area, make sure he is cute and cuddly—NEVER a menacing animal). Actually, it has been said (in many traditions) that by placing pictures of babies and baby animals all around your home you will attract your very own baby there as well.

Extra Ellen Advice
(From Experience and the Archives, Too!)

• NEVER vacuum under the bed while you are trying to get pregnant. In Eastern cultures they believe that the *ling* (or soul) of your child circles your bed in its efforts to get to you. That includes trying to get your attention from down under it. Don't sweep or vacuum under your bed until after your sweet one has come and is sleeping in his or her own space. Try, though, to clear all clutter from under your bed before you begin any efforts at conception. (Explanation above.)

• Never put any fertility symbols in the bathroom. Their fortune gets flushed away with all your attempts.

• BELIEVE in yourself, in these cures, and, mostly, in your baby's ability to find you. BELIEVE. BELIEVE. And then believe some more because this stuff really does work.

A Personal P.S.

Right before I became pregnant with my son, I was so tenacious about this agenda that even when I traveled I brought green sheets with me to sleep on. My family and friends thought I was certifiable. But I had heard amazing success stories accorded to the green-sheet thing.

On one particular trip I had gone to visit my sister with my hopes, green sheets, and credit cards. Those days were chock-FULL of retail therapy. Anyway, I guess we had done a little too much shopping because I needed to borrow a small suitcase to carry "stuff" home (okay, okay, I bought a stuffed tiger at FAO Schwarz while on Fifth Avenue in New York City . . . there, I fessed up).

When I returned home and was unpacking my gear, I found a small silver baby comb at the bottom of the borrowed suitcase. I, OF COURSE, took this as an omen (c'mon, it IS me!) and a sign that my little bundle was sending me a message and that soon enough he would deliver it to me literally live and in person. I called my sister, who knew nothing about the comb, and she said I could keep it (AS IF she were getting it back anyway!). I had already started to prep a room in our condo as a nursery (there's that critical air of expectancy), and I hung that comb in the Children/Creativity area of the room. Right next to the brand-new cuddly stuffie tiger.

Three days later, my fertility specialist called while he was vacationing on a ski trip in Colorado to tell me I was pregnant with a strong and healthy baby. He delivered the good news, I delivered the happy, healthy boy, but I still don't know who delivered the comb.

I'll let you decide.

ITTY-BITTY BABY SHUI

These LUCKY little cures or adjustments honor the BIRTH day of a new baby's life. Whenever a new member of the global tribe enters this world, whether biologically or adopted, our entire orbit suddenly starts to spin completely differently and every little detail of our lives takes on a whole new BIG meaning. Suddenly, there is this amazing little being totally dependent on us for survival. The reality is that becoming a parent can be hugely overwhelming and even sometimes scary—while simultaneously being one of the best times of our lives and truly a cause for celebration.

By the time you bring your little bundle of joy home, I'm sure you have prepared a wonderful, warm, and welcoming space for her. But even if this environment is the sweetest, cutest, and cuddliest place in the whole wide world, your baby comes with her own distinct nature and energies (which she seems to have no problem letting everyone around her know about), and these trappings are then ushered into the house with your baby's arrival. This baby energy is powerful and, yes, actually DOES affect her new space along with yours. You've all seen or heard about it before: Her baby is so calm and joyful while her sister's baby might be A LOT more sensitive to the energies all around. It's strictly a result of their itty-bitty individual DNA, and never a reflection of your parenting skills!

Whatever the case may be with your own wee one, you can both celebrate and add comfort to your newborn's entrance into this world by following some or all of these LUCKY DAY cures:

- Ancient custom holds that if a child receives a red shirt on the day he is born, the "yang," or strong, nature of that garment will strengthen his immune system while additionally helping to acclimate his energy from womb to room. This red shirt will bring luck and good fortune to any baby while also supporting a healthy and playful atmosphere. Note that the shirt need not actually be worn to have these wondrous effects, but, rather, can just as easily be placed anywhere in the Children/Creativity area of the house, or, more naturally, in this same sector of the newborn's room.

• This lucky child can also receive what Feng Shui calls the "Gift of Light." This gift will crystallize and invite more playful and peaceful energies along with health and happiness into baby's room, because, well, what child could have too much of any and all of those energies? You invite the Gift of Light by attaching a small, round, faceted crystal to nine inches of red ribbon, string, thread, or yarn and hanging it in any window of the child's room. This "crystal cure" will bring along with it kindness, warmth, stability, and serenity to both your child and her environs.

• As caretakers we are always vigilant and concerned for our children's safety. Let's face it, we just cannot be around to watch them 24–7, as much as our hearts and our thoughts may try to do so. LUCKILY (uh-huh!), besides taking everyday precautions, there is also a Feng Shui baby-proofing adjustment that is thought to help ward off accident, illness, injury, and disease. For this you will need a white and rounded candle (it can be as tall as a pillar candle or as tiny as a tea light), which you will then light and let burn for the first seven days of baby's life. The candle need not burn all the way down; it's only necessary for the wick to engage the wax and get a bit of a flame going in order for the baby to elicit the promised energies. And here's a BONUS: In case you missed the window of the first seven days of life, you can perform this very same cure on any birthday and the six days following it.

Quick Decorating Tips for Newborns

- Feng Shui suggests using pale yellow as THE color to decorate the nursery, as this will help support a spirit of cheerfulness as well as imitating the life-affirming qualities of the Sun. I (strongly) warn against using a propensity of ANY primary colors, such as bright reds or oranges, as they will often be much too stimulating for an infant. It's better to save these colors for a room where activity is encouraged, such as a playroom or living room.

- For a colicky or sensitive baby, add some blue to the nursery or anywhere the baby spends lots of time; light blues and greens offer a calming, de-stressing effect whether the baby is a boy or a girl.

- Contrary to pop-culture decor, NEVER hang a mobile (or anything moving, for that matter) over the baby's face or head. Anything that hangs above their head is both scary to and for them. As well, keep the furnishings and the decorations in the nursery to a minimum for at least the first few months of their little lives. Remember, all this little soul has seen for the last nine months is a lot of amniotic fluid. Big lions and huge giraffes are better off in the jungle, where they belong!

- Stimulate your new baby's Chi by hanging a tinkling metal wind chime in the nursery window.

- If the baby is now sleeping in a room that once upon a time had another purpose, make sure to ring a bell all around the room to clean and clear any stuck or stagnant energies from the past. This new little one (life, that is) needs to have a space he can call his very own. Try to bang a gong before you actually move any furniture into the room, and, obviously, before you move the baby in. You might also want to follow some tried-and-true traditions and place a bowl of sea salt in this space before baby is brought home, as this will also absorb and negate any leftover conflicted or harmful energies that might be hanging around the room.

CHRISTENING OR BABY-NAMING CEREMONY

Regardless of religious or even cultural background, almost every tradition on the planet has a way of celebrating the birth of a child that includes the involvement of extended family. This rite of passage not only engages the parents but usually strongly leans on support from grandparents, siblings, godparents, and, well, the list goes on. Christians mark this new beginning with a christening. Jews celebrate both the bris, a religious ritual that centers around a baby boy's circumcision, and a naming ceremony for infant girls. Most traditions celebrate a new addition to

"If this child thrives under your devoted care, may its face shine. May it uproot nightshade with its brushing thigh. May it not become ill."
—*West African prayer to protect the newborn*

the family tree with a fabulous feast following their custom of choice.

Even with all their inherent beauty and bounty, these bitty souls can sometimes face some very big challenges, so, no matter how fragile or fierce these fighting little infants are, these babies need our oversight and protection, and, of course, can always benefit from some LUCKY Baby Shui.

Next come some cures that will enhance our invitation to incorporate this new little life into our own and the lives of all those around us whom we love and value. Some of these adjustments come straight from the cradle of Shui, while others branch out from other cultural customs and traditions, but they are all, each and every one, meant to bring Health, Happiness, and Prosperity (the Three Great Blessings in Feng Shui) to the newest member of our society.

- Gift the newborn with some sort of lucky charm (and I'm not talking about marshmallow hearts here, either!). It is widely held that the effects of giving a child something considered lucky will be both balancing and harmonizing from the conscious as well as the subconscious perspective. It connects the child on an invisible, advantageous, and etheric level with all things fortunate and lucky. Some examples that fit this bill include miniature pianos and harps (angelic protection), teapots (I can only guess that this came from Ireland, but I do know it's supposed to bring luck to the baby), bells (to ward off negative spirits), shoes (to walk proudly through this life), boats (for smooth sailing), keys, turtles, tortoises, birds (to soar with flights of fancy and many freedoms), and the moon and stars. Other charms include a money clip (abundance), or symbols like violins, butterflies, swans, and fairies. Whether given as a single slice of fortune and luck or placed upon a bracelet full of charms, any or all of these items will bring the baby all the best these intentions have to offer.

Baby-Naming Benefit

A "traditional" christening bracelet has a padlock on it to lock in good fortune and luck.

• When issuing invites for the child's christening or naming celebration, go ahead and decorate the invitations with any of the aforementioned lucky charms (this can be a sticker, imprint, or actual graphic illustration) and be sure to use the appropriate and age-old associative colors of blue for boy and pink for girl. If this sounds old-fashioned it should because it's actually ancient, but go ahead and indulge yourselves here—for some age-old luck!

• Sending faux plastic eggs, manufactured in the color of the planned festivities (you can even stuff the invites inside the eggs), underscores the miracle of fertility and lends luck and fortune to the event—again, blue for boys, pink for girls.

• Suggest that the guests might even want to add to the panache by wearing these same colors to celebrate opening night. Now, this doesn't mean that Uncle Sol needs to drag out his old blue leisure suit, but he can wear a beautiful blue Brooks Brothers tie as he goes to his great-grand-nephew's naming. Using a touch of color honors the child and indicates true inclusion in the ceremony.

• If there are godparents participating in the event, then each of them should, individually, receive their own special photo of this special child with all the baby's pertinent data (date and place of birth, weight, height, endearing qualities and characteristics—jeez, if I had done this, I would have needed a poster!) written on the back. Make sure to write the names of BOTH godparents on the back of these photos so that these very special people remain forever bonded in their task of together supporting and loving this child.

• Ask anyone considered a grandma to tie a nine-inch piece of red ribbon, string, thread, or yarn anywhere on the baby's crib to bring protection, peace, and precious nana-love to her precious cargo. Traditionally, each grandmother would tie one piece of ribbon on one foot of the crib, suggesting her willingness to help this child walk sweetly with her grand-motherly support through his lifetime.

• Tradition also says that this new little addition to the family tree should get one of his or her own . . . a tree, that is! Plant-ing pine trees to "give back" for the gift of a baby boy will bring to him strength of character, courage, and longevity (every-thing that this tree and your son possesses!). Cherry trees are planted to welcome our sweet little girls and, it is said, will bring to them a lightness of being and a lifetime of joy and purity. It's that pure; it's that simple. These trees can be planted in the garden of a grandparent, in the yard of the house where the child lives, or in any public arena that will allow for such plant-ings. It is additionally believed that these trees, as they thrive and grow, will also lend the child vitality and immunity to child-hood diseases. These beliefs have come down through the ages and grown in popularity in recent times.

• Another good-luck suggestion that some parents find useful is to send a "wish list" before the celebration so that four thousand silver Tiffany spoons in tiny blue boxes don't arrive, with nary a necessary and needed new nappie bag in sight!

• There are many customs that find that luck happens when the first name of the child begins with the alphabetical letter that precedes the one that begins the last name (surname). For instance, my maiden name is Drury, beginning with the letter D. If my parents had known and practiced this LUCKY tradition, then my first name should have begun with a C, like my very luckily named cousin, Cathy Drury. This is thought to create an energetically smooth and flowing pathway through life.

• Whatever you name your child will literally impact and influence his or her destiny, so be sure to take her own nature into account before pinning any moniker on her. If you have a sensitive, quiet child who seems to withdraw from loud noises and clowns climbing out of small cars, "P.T." probably won't cut it. And, please, no matter how sweet and ethereal your little wonder may be, Fluffy, Muffy, and Puffy are all names for cats. Period.

• Placing a sprig of fresh rosemary under the baby's pillow until it is completely dried out is thought to bring him sweet dreams for all of his days and, more important in the early going, for his nights as well

• Any gift of silver or gold given to the child is considered more valuable or meaningful than giving toys and/or clothes. Bangles, baubles, and even gold coins wish the child a life of ease and grace and, specifically, abundance from every arena.

And now my personal favorite lucky charm of all, for all our little loved ones:

- Tie nine Chinese coins on red ribbon, string, thread, or yarn and hang this symbol behind where the head of the baby rests while she is sleeping. Tie it anywhere on the crib. This cure is said to empower the child with virtues and gifts and the individual qualities of a perfected being . . . just like EVERY single one of them is. It is also believed to keep the baby from any and all danger.

And that particular last fact is why this is my particular favorite.

FIRST DAY OF SCHOOL SHUI

One of my clients recently called me as she readied herself—and her daughter—for the FIRST DAY OF SCHOOL. It was the end of summer and her daughter, Grace, was soon to enter kindergarten—"The Big K," as Mom called it. "I can remember my daughter's first day of preschool as if it were yesterday. Now she's entering kindergarten and I'm an absolute basket case! I don't know whether to prep her or just send her off and hope for the best."

Now, this conundrum is as old as the hills—parents getting crazy nervous about sending their kids off to school. We all seem to go through the same jitters whether our kids are two, ten, or twenty-one! The first day of school is just one of those days that calls for a bit of planning.

One of the first things I always recommend to my nervous parent clients is that they should (read: MUST!) try, about two weeks before school begins, to get their kids back into some sort

Naming Baby

So many societies hold such strong beliefs regarding the naming of a child that one can see the tremendous implications this sacred duty implies. Most traditions hold that the child MUST be named by the seventh day after his birth. For centuries the English believed that a butterfly was the flying soul of a child who had died before she had been named. Customarily, it is considered mandatory to name the child in order to connect his soul (*ling*) or Chi to this realm, this earth. The name is therefore connected to a child's whole being—physical, emotional, mental, and spiritual. This name will therefore root her, planting her firmly here in our world, where she now belongs. In a sense, then, a baby's name can give magical and powerfully protective qualities.

Tibetans name their children after the day of the week on which they are born. Hawaiians name their children after something that happened or was witnessed around the same time of their birth. The Aborigines in Australia start to recite a list of names and don't stop until the placenta pops out, at which point they stop and recognize that they have their name. Good thing I'm not Aboriginal, or my son's name would be "MORE PERCOCET!!!"

Shakespeare had it going on when he said, "A rose by any other name . . ."

Be conscious that whatever name the baby is given will help to create what the rest of his days will hold for him. Your part is to bless your child with the gift of *conscious* baby naming.

Celebrating Childhood

Just as we have celebrations and rituals that mark the birth of a new member of our family tree, so do many cultures and traditions also have similarly themed events that herald the growth of these new branches. In effect, we all continue to celebrate childhood every step of the way, in all different ways.

One of the most wonderful traditions has to do with baby's first steps. After all, there aren't many more moments in those first few years of your baby's life that elicit more excitement than when your little one exhibits his or her first shot, or step, into individual independence. Traditionally, the most cautious parents (especially those who have an ancestral heritage in the East) will be sure to walk behind the child during this first foray into the world of walking and they will cut the cord that they believe continued to bind the baby to the netherworld of Spirit. These Oriental traditions maintain that there are invisible bindings that are tied around the ankles of the child. That is, until they begin to take their first steps. Therefore, it is customary for someone from the child's family to walk behind and cut three invisible lines into the ground after the baby takes his or her first steps; this symbolically cuts that cord and will allow the child to roam freely forever more. Just beautiful.

of ritual and routine that will mimic their school schedule. Waiting until the final twenty-four hours usually won't bear fruit, unless you're talking about stomping grapes and then drinking fermented ones to help quell your own jangling nerves.

Here, then, is my tried, true, and really, really *tested* First Day of School LUCKY DAY Shui:

Back to School LUCKY DAY Shui

Returning to school—at age eight or eighteen—can always stir up some stress. Here's some simple advice for making your child's transition a whole lot easier and a whole lot less stressful. It's critical to note that a child's room really can impact his or her study habits, for better or for worse, and will have an influential effect on grades as well (obviously of more interest to the older kids). A child's environment, regardless of age, can create great supportive energies as they navigate both emotional and social growth.

• Place a globe (any size) of the world in their Knowledge and Self-Cultivation area (lower left-hand corner of his or her bedroom) to promote and sustain healthy social growth and interest in worldly affairs. This symbol of the globe will also help to ground your child.

• By placing a globe inside this space (the Knowledge *gua*) you are also bringing great Chi to your child's academic development and supporting his or her school achievements. Believe me, I've seen Ds turn to Bs as quickly as you could turn a globe around when this cure was enacted with these specific scholarly intentions.

• Put some recognition in your child's Achievement sector (similar to the adult Fame arena); it's so important and special for parents to let their kids know they see and are proud of what and how they are doing. Display such things as their artwork, trophies, merit awards, or highly graded papers.

• Add educational artwork or maps to this same space (or, really, anywhere in a child's room) to foster a sense of wonder and childlike curiosity.

- Place your child's bed in the "command position" of the room (so that the child is facing the door, not behind or on the side of it). Further empower him by making sure that he has some access to turning on a light, whether that be a small bedside lamp or the ability to reach and activate an overhead light. This gives a child a great sense of security, power, and control, just as sleeping in that "command position" does.
- Use the pastel tones of blues and greens to create a unifying theme throughout your children's rooms. If you have a little princess, she will benefit from a light shade of pink as well. It simply cannot be stated enough that primary colors should be saved for spaces meant to stimulate. Until a child is in her mid-teens, her energies are considered unstable and, for all obvious reasons, undeveloped.
- Children between the ages of fifteen and their mid-twenties truly benefit from a more serene and stable environment in their bedrooms. For this reason, make sure that their furniture, furnishings, and all other accoutrements are fairly heavy and solid, and not moved around the room (as in constantly redecorating) too much.
- Smaller children need more spacious rooms and smaller furniture. They need room to grow and space for activity. Big, heavy pieces of furniture can actually have a harmful effect on them, dwarfing their progress and their dreams. In fact, Feng Shui maintains that large pieces of furniture in any child's bedroom can oppress their Chi and even lead to broken bones if placed too close to the door!

• Two weeks before school is set to begin, start to wake your children closer to the time that they will be rising and (hopefully!) shining for the first school bell. This will most likely require an earlier bedtime, which will, in turn, help to support the institution and encouragement of patterns, rituals, and routines—all of which kids absolutely, literally, thrive on.

• Use the power of scent, specifically a blend of lavender and chamomile, at night to calm your kids and help keep them quiet and happy. Put ten drops of each of these (100 percent) essential oils in a spray bottle and then fill with distilled water. Spritz this sleepy-time spray around their rooms at night to give the sandman a huge helping hand. Put a few drops in their nightly bath or even drop a couple into the washing machine while doing their laundry. Then, when school starts, you can spray their backpacks and clothes so that throughout the day they will have a scentual reminder of home and hearth. For the smaller set, you can shake a few drops on a cotton ball or hankie and pin it on their clothes somewhere, always reminding them that home is just a wee whiff away. You should try to begin using these oils at least three weeks before school starts to set the pattern and also to induce the calm and peace presented and promised by these oily little miracle workers.

HALLOWEEN

Goblins and ghosts and . . . Shui? Yes, as sure as Shui, this is the day where nothing is as it seems, neither trick nor treat nor fright nor light. Spirits are said to wander and roam and even try to cause a bit of autumn mischief. And with all this potential for misbegotten magic hanging heavy in the air, Halloween is the perfect time to offer a big amount of protection to our little Hershey hustlers.

Here's a little LUCKY DAY Shui advice that's heavy on the protection and light on both the pocketbook and the worry load. Some of this takes a bit of preplanning, so give yourself a little extra time so as not to get too scared to run out of it:

• Have your little fairy or action hero don her favorite T-shirt or pajama shirt UNDERNEATH her costume. This inner layer of safety will keep your children feeling much more secure as they face the outer demons, and, take it from me, they will far less likely be wandering your halls at three AM looking for Mom or Dad to check under the bed for the zillionth time that night.

• Costumes are notorious for being "too scratchy" or just plain uncomfortable. So if you pair that aforementioned T-shirt or pajama with favorite jeans or matching pj bottoms, then you will not only help to prevent a flood of fears from overflowing their little psyches but you will, as before, create a subtle but true sense of security. It's almost as if they are wearing their favorite blankie or stuffed animal, keeping something FAMILIAR, warm, and cozy against their skin as they haul their sugar from one house to the next. Keep in mind, as well, that the softer the fabric and the lighter the color of the clothes UNDER their costume, the more balance there is to offset the symbolic darkness of this holiday.

• Be sure the kids eat something before heading out for the evening haunt. We know they're excited thinking about their bounty and booty and which friends they will play what tricks on, but they need something nutritious in their little systems to offset the sugar overload that's heading their way. As we have all found out (usually the hard way), sugar on an empty stomach is an invitation for a headache. That pounding they hear won't be little Bobby next door looking for his loot, but rather a knock on their noggin that will put them in a baaaaaad mood. Dinner becomes crucial. It can be light, easy to prepare, and just as easy to eat. Anything from pizza to peanut butter and jelly with a piece of fresh fruit (or veggies) will absolutely do the job.

• Set some Spook Rules that EVERYONE AGREES UPON:

  • Contract on the curfew.

  • Agree beforehand on the amount of candy that can be eaten that night. (And then throw in two extra pieces for good measure. After all, it is Halloween!)

  • If you have more than one child, create a set place where each of the kids can keep their stash that is theirs and theirs alone. Believe me, they know EXACTLY how many mini Baby Ruths they got, and as far as they're concerned, they own 'em!

  • Make sure the house is really well lit and peaceful so that as these tired trick-or-treaters return home, they walk toward a beacon of comfort. Soft and/or familiar music playing in the background also helps to soften the vibe and create a feeling of safety and security. For all their bravado, our little munchkins need to know there'll be no more foolish ghoulish ghosting going on once they're through the door and getting ready for bed. They are home. And they are safe. And they aren't Spider-Man anymore.

• As we know, Feng Shui is really big on "clearing the clutter," and candy counts here, too! This is a wonderful opportunity to teach our kids the lesson of sharing—clearing the candy clutter both inside and out. We always put aside some booty to give to those who may remain costumeless. Local old-age homes, soup kitchens, and shelters are always happy to receive the excess, and, BONUS, the kids see that their actions have consequences—in this case, of the sweetest kind.

• If there is one night to use lavender and chamomile essential oils in their baths along with sprinkling or spritzing a few drops on their pillows or sheets, Halloween is IT! Their little nerves, as well as your bigger ones, might be a little frayed by the end of this day, so using three to six drops of each in their bathwater or adding same amount to a spray bottle of distilled water will calm and curb those last efforts at getting "just one more lollipop . . . please????"

IT'S SWEET MUSIC TO YOUR EARS

Music has always been known to lift the spirits and salve the soul as well as soothe the savage beast. But recently, science actually supported a unique way to harness the power of this creative energy as well as connect you to all of yours. A few years ago a private university completed a double-blind study that scientifically supported the power of Feng Shui to empower the creative impulses we all have waiting in the wings to take flight.

It was a small study in which sixty or so septuagenarians (people who are seventy-plus years old) were asked to listen to some of their favorite music from their youth. Think "Don't Sit Under the Apple Tree" and other saucy melodies from many, many years gone by. Before actually sitting down and doing the listening, they were divided into two groups, with one group placing the source of the music in the Knowledge and Self-Cultivation sector of their Bagua and the other half placing the source of the music in the Children and Creativity sector of the homes.

They were then advised to listen to the music every day for twenty-seven days. They played it continually. The upshot of the study was this: The people who listened to their favorite childhood tunes in their Knowledge and Self-Cultivation sector experienced virtually no changes but had a lot of good memories, while those who listened to their tunes in Children and Creativity experienced visceral and real physiological and emotional transformations. Some people experienced not only a decrease in cholesterol and blood sugar, but also elevations in mood and in many other barometers of increased health—mental, physical, and emotional!

So if you're interested in opening yourself to the beauty and the power of music to trigger your own creative impulses, follow this wonderful cure by putting any musical instrument, musical symbol, or representation of music in your Children and Creativity sector. This could mean a boom box, a Victrola, a CD player, or even your iPod. Try this for twenty-seven days to activate the cure. Music played here stimulates harmonies and melodies in all your creative endeavors.

WORDS OF INSPIRATION

For those of us in creative fields, it's no surprise that our wells of inspiration occasionally run dry. Who hasn't heard of the infamous writer's block? Thank heavens there is a fast and easy way to refill these reservoirs and motivate those muses. A client,

...iel, who works a day job as a bank manager but whose life-long dream is to finish and publish a thriller novel recently used this potent cure, and he has not only finished his first effort but has already found an interested agent!

Here's the cure to attract creative inspiration:

1. Create a color sequence made of nine three-inch pieces of ribbon, string, thread, or yarn or any other kind of fabric or paper in all the colors of the Bagua. The color sequence

The Color Purple

You can use the color cure for many inspirational purposes, depending on which energy of the Bagua you want to activate. My client Nora, a visual artist, came to me to help her activate her Wealth energy. She desperately needed to sell more of her artwork or she was at risk of losing her studio space. So when she created her color sequence using the thread, she began her efforts with the color purple, to activate Wealth energies. But, lo and behold, after watching in temporary relief and satisfaction as she saw a few of her biggest paintings leave her studio under the arms of happy buyers, she began to feel completely blocked creatively, unable to produce any new work. Frustrated and nervous, she contacted me again. I simply suggested she begin the color cure again, this time beginning with the color white—to activate and inspire her creative juices. Seven months later, Nora is not only thriving financially but also feeling unbelievably creative and happy with all her efforts!

needs to begin with the color of the energy that you are attempting to activate. In this case, you want to kick up your
creativity, so you begin with white, as that is the color associated with the energy of Children and Creativity. You then
attach (or tie) the eight successive colors of the Bagua in
their order (moving around the Bagua in a clockwise direction) and end with the color that immediately precedes the
one that began the whole endeavor.

2. Take a piece of white poster board or a white dry-erase
board and place or hang the color sequence on the white
background. Place the entire piece in your Children and
Creativity sector.

	8	
Wealth and Prosperity	Fame and Reputation	Relationship, Romance, and Marriage
Family, Friends, and Ancestors	Health	Children and Creativity
Knowledge and Self-Cultivation	Career	**Helpful People and Travel**

NO MAN IS an island entirely to him- (or her-) self, but if you cast a net—the one called Helpful People and Travel—upon your own personal waters, you simply won't believe the number of friends, benefactors, and really plugged-in connections that can quickly come swimming your way. From far and wide, your net of support will become stronger and deeper, bringing in some pretty big fish, too! There will be so many people who will want to pool their intentions with yours that you'll just be amazed. It's true. No matter how hard or how often we work, we pray, we cry, and we try, we all, every one of us, sometimes feel like we're swimming upstream and could use someone to give us a good tug toward shore. We need people to pull us up by our bootstraps, or, in the case of some really skinny boots (the kind without side zippers), sometimes we just need somebody else to help pull 'em off. (Oh, there I go with personal stories from my own boot camp!)

The Lucky Shui in this section will help you find your guides and guidance, support and boundaries—all in one fell swoop. You'll find that some of your Helpful People live right around the corner while others might actually live most of their lives in the spotlight. And just wait and see, a few might not actually have both feet on this planet, but they certainly have both eyes, along with their hearts and souls (invisible or not), as well as all their prayers and invisible efforts, pointed in your direction.

And speaking of direction, this is also the sector to be addressed when you want to travel to destinations unknown, or even ones you've been to before but have been dreaming about revisiting forever.

According to ancient dictate, this place called Helpful People/ Travel (pretty self-explanatory, don't you think?) is located in the lower right-hand corner of your home, bedroom, living room, office, or any other space in which you spend a lot of time. Always when we activate or trigger the energies of this area, they not only influence our tendencies toward traveling (whether literally or on some other, greater path in our lives or careers) but also associate us with charity, philanthropy, and our own not-to-be-crossed boundaries. Isn't that enough reason to keep it in balance and of "benefit"?

This area belongs to the metal element, so the colors we attribute to it are grays, golds, and silvers (metallics). So if you are looking to invite all the help the Universe possibly has to offer or just to get the heck out of Dodge, this is the space to take a good, hard look at. (And speaking of Dodge, don't worry, I even included your car trips in this Travel section as well!) The number accorded to Helpful People and Travel is 6—so six symbols that touch your head, heart, or soul (statues of angels?) or the names of six principal people, written one at a time and placed in this arena, will bring instant and immediate networking rewards.

Take some inspiration from the suggestions below and remember that the most helpful person you know is usually standing right in front of your mirror staring back at you. But on those days when your eyes are a little cloudy, help yourself to these Helpful People advisos.

MARTIN LUTHER KING, JR., DAY

As I looked over the list of Special Days that I would be covering in this book, some of them stuck out like especially black-and-blue sore thumbs. Of course, what a great idea to have a unique and wondrous baby shower that presages health and happiness and a lucky little life not only for the baby but for the parents as well. Or how terrific to be able to share knowledge of tried-and-tested customs and traditions that will help to make someone's next family gathering one for the record books and/or twelve-hundred-dollar laptop photo album.

When I looked at the list and came across Martin Luther King, Jr., Day, I thought, and I'm being brutally honest here, Well, I'm not black and I really haven't "experienced" that struggle, although many of my very good friends have. And though I certainly respect and look up to this icon of American history as an adult, I didn't grow up with a complete understanding of who he was or what he was trying to do with his brief life and peaceful mission on this planet. No, as a family when I was growing up, we had portraits, paintings, and pictures of President John F. Kennedy, Pope John, and, of course, the obligatory oils of all four of the kids in my family displayed around the living room. But no Martin Luther King, Jr.

So as I pondered this Special Day, I figured I would make it a sort of quick read about putting some peace plans into place and that would be that.

But then something happened inside me. I started to research Dr. King and his quest, and I began to think of all the ways his philosophies attempted to impact a Universe screaming for his slant, a planet of people who for ages have killed the messenger without ever really trying their hardest to implement the message. Suddenly, Martin Luther King, Jr., Day became, for me, the most important Special Day of all because this celebration of his birthday and his message is all about peace, truth, and fairness—in our homes, our hearts, our lives, our communities, and then, collectively, on this earth. Indeed, once I truly took in the meaning of this man, his work, and his life, I realized that Dr. King embodied the essence of what I try to do every day—in my business and in my practice—and what I try to inspire in others.

I also realized that it was as if this man has been inspiring me all along. So in writing this Special Day, it became my mission to honor this day, to honor this man, and, most of all, to honor what he tried to tell us. So here goes.

Consider just this little glimpse into the pain and the experience of the human condition that I hear as regularly as I can hear my heartbeat if I quiet my mind, hold my breath, and blow hard while pinching my nose shut, and see if any of this beats AT ALL true for you:

"My spouse never listens to a word I say!"

"My kids are fighting constantly!"

"My boss is such an @*%&%(^."

"There's a bully on my son's bus."

"My ex hasn't paid support in years."

"I don't get nearly the money I deserve at work."

Battered wives, abusive husbands, divorce, oppression, negativity, racism, poverty, TERRORISM! This all starts INSIDE US and travels outward, reaping its ugly harvest each and every time any one of us has an ugly thought or strikes out at another human being. No matter what the reason or the excuse, the insanity begins within each and every one of us. Dr. King once said, "Everything that we see is a shadow cast by that which we do not see." He was talking about the energy all around us. He was talking about using that which is all around us to get our own selves up the mountain, the one that he saw that has peace and prosperity on the other side. He had a dream. You have many. Let's begin to blend the two here, on this Special Day.

When I begin a consultation, I always start with the same ideal, saying the same thing for the same reason: "Peace within, peace without." From my client Teena, who called me because her son was being deployed to Iraq and she wanted to do something from her home that could "bring peace to this planet and protect him at the same time," to Janet, whose husband "had beaten her for the last time" and who needed desperately to learn new ways to bring balance and identity to her existence. Each and every client is essentially asking me for the same thing: peace—peace of mind, peace in their lives, and just peace period. And that peace can begin in your bedroom.

You should make your bedroom a sanctuary, where you will both begin and end your day with loving, helpful, and happy thoughts. Because if this is the energy that you exude, then this, too, will be the energy you contribute to making your world, the one we all walk around in with you, a much better place to be.

By the way, before we begin some suggestions to put that peace into place, let me share the upshot of the aforementioned two stories. The day after I consulted with Teena, the concerned and worried mom, the Baker Report was released and the Democrats had just taken over Congress. This may seem coincidental, but you never know. And although her "career army" and precious only son is still training and stationed at Fort Benning, it doesn't appear that he'll have to go anyplace sandy real soon. And Janet finally stopped buying into the idea that she was a victim to her husband's abuse and violence, and has left him and that horrific life behind.

MAKE YOUR BEDROOM A PEACE-FILLED SANCTUARY (AND THEN MAKE THE WHOLE WORLD A BETTER PLACE)

- Your bedroom should be your refuge and a place to promote deep sleep, deep thinking, and deep dreaming. You should always look forward to entering this space as somewhere that will allow you to experience peace and bliss and tap into your consciousness so that you may not only listen to that "still, small voice within" but also that you might act on it as well.

· Using the many shades of blue and green all around you in the space in which you sleep both soothes and heals the soul and the spirit. This could be from the paint on the walls to the color of the accessories you have hanging around your room. There have been studies and research showing that these two hues, both green and blue, will bring balance and beauty to your sleep time and your thoughts, which is why hospitals and other institutions of health and healing use these colors both on the exterior and in the apparel (think the color of surgical scrubs). You do want these colors to be pale in nature, though. Big, bold primary colors don't lend themselves to a quiet, receptive mind.

· Ideally there should be no water in the bedroom. Even in pictures. Water stimulates, and even though it is considered a yin, or quiet, energy, it simply is not appropriate for the bedroom. Besides, I have had plenty of clients tell me that they tried to put fountains in the Wealth area of their bedroom but ended up having to go to the bathroom all night long.

· If you are either recovering from an illness OR have A LOT of electronic equipment in this room, then you should also have some healthy green plants there to both offer their oxygen as life sustenance as well as absorb the radiation stemming from the electromagnetic frequencies (EMFs). Even the magnetic frequencies emitted by the lights on the alarm clock that sits on the bedside table right next to your head can cause anything from unexplained headaches to an unwillingness to face the day with a positive attitude. Place a live green plant in the line of fire between you and your clock and let it absorb the negativity, giving you a positive night's sleep.

• If you are recovering from a *serious* illness, you should have anywhere from nine to eleven fresh green plants growing in your room. But this is ONLY if you are recovering or recuperating. Otherwise, generally, the energy emanating from live plants is too "aggressive" for the bedroom and is better used in other spaces of the home or office to help facilitate or oxygenate your Chi.

• Too many pillows crowd and cramp the bed. You need space—to think, to move about, and to dream. Two pillows per person is the standard.

• At least once every two years (if not more often), clear out under the bed and inside your closet. Give clothes away that others might make better use of. This definitely creates great Karma for you and contributes to making our planet more plentiful and peace-filled.

• Around your bedroom, feature pictures of people, places, or things that speak to or capture peace and feelings of Universal hope, protection, and security. Angels in the Helpful People section (lower right-hand area) or symbols or pictures of icons like Dr. King in that same space will subtly remind you that the peace you hold in your heart lends itself to finding that same principle on this planet. Anything that depicts ferocious animals or anything that simulates war (you would not believe how many clients I have who display swords or weapons of destruction) will contribute to an outward expression of violence and/or war, whether it's a personal one with your slob of a roommate or something on a more global scale. You want to keep it sweet in the slumber spot.

• If you have created a work space in your bedroom, it needs to be sectioned off somehow (possibly behind a small screen) or you risk taking your work to bed with you and never tapping into other opportunities and potentials that are waiting for you when you close your eyes and relax. You need to allow these inspirations to find their way into your psyche.

• Exercise equipment in the bedroom comes with the same codicil as the work space caution. Most indoor exercise equipment allows you the cardio component, but the truth is you never really get anywhere. You can run ten miles up a steep and sweat-producing hill, but at the end you're still two steps from the comforter that lies across the bottom of the bed. The implication here is that you are moving all the time but never really gaining any momentum.

• Wooden headboards will serve you better than metal ones. Again, this goes back to that whole EMF thing. Metal is a magnetic conductor. Wood quiets and quells any and all electronic energy circulating around your room. But if you do have metal surrounding you while you sleep, put red felt "feet" around the legs of the bed (see sidebar below.)

• Resolve conflicts and bring harmony to house and home, but reflect and resolve the same inside yourself. The Hawaiians call this Ho'oponopono, and it is a gift their Huna philosophy has given the world that literally means "to set relationships right." It is a long and somewhat complicated process of healing but essentially says the same thing we have been honoring Dr. King for here. Examine right relationships in yourself. Take responsibility for your own thoughts and actions. Don't gossip. Wish all others well, especially those who push your buttons the most. Bless them unconditionally and often. Literally "see" how all others mirror your own feelings, then recognize how you contribute to the conflict and how you can resolve the conflict. If only inside yourself. By changing YOU, you can change the world both inside and out. "YOU must be the change you wish to see in the world." Gandhi certainly got that right!

Sleep in Heavenly Peace

- It's critical to remember that what you think about as you fall off to sleep, as well as what your first thoughts are in the morning, influences and creates your attitudes and opportunities for the whole of the day. Get into the HABIT of affirming something positive and desired to yourself right before you fall asleep and as soon as you awake. As Goethe said, "Whatever you can do, or dream you can, begin it. Boldness has genius, power, and magic in it." And you can create that just by changing your thoughts, therefore changing your mind, in the habit-forming twenty-seven-day period. Pick ANY affirmation, such as "Health, Happiness, and Prosperity," and say it silently as you go to sleep and then as soon as you wake up. Some days I wake up and spontaneously say "Today's MY Lucky Day," and then, of course, it is. Try it, it works.

- Take four pieces of red felt and cut them each about an inch larger than the feet on your bed. First place one under each individual foot, and then pull them up and tie them around each foot—this will ground your energies while you sleep at night, and, according to ancient Eastern customs and traditions, will keep you safe, warm, and very well protected while your soul makes peace with your psyche.

- To protect home and family, put any earthenware container (ceramic, terra-cotta, glass, crystal—something natural, from the earth, see?) and fill to 70 percent with uncooked rice. Take seven small clear quartz crystals and place them in an arrow formation atop the rice with the tip of the arrow pointing toward the top of the bed or where your head lies. Place this under your bed on the side that you sleep on, beneath where your heart rests when you are fully prone. If it makes you more comfortable, cover the container with clear plastic wrap, or leave it uncovered for full effect. This "arrow" keeps you protected from anything that goes bump in the night.

Lao Tze, the philosopher who is credited with many of Feng Shui's theories and practices, once said:

> *If there is right in the soul,*
> *There will be beauty in the person.*
> *If there is beauty in the person,*
> *There will be harmony in the home.*
> *If there is harmony in the home,*
> *There will be order in the nation.*
> *If there is order in the nation,*
> *There will be peace in the world.*

I wish you order in your nation and honor you for creating peace in the world. It is what Martin Luther King, Jr., thought, taught, and died for. But I'll just bet he honors you for your efforts, too!

PRESIDENTS' DAY

Winter blahs. One of the perfect prescriptions for these postholiday blues is a long weekend that includes an extra day to sleep in. So, it seems, just for me, someone decided to cram two of my favorite presidents' birthdays into one holiday in February when we get to sleep late and then think about what it must be like to be president. Or, at least sleep late. And I was only kidding when I said it was just for me. Of course, we are encouraged to remember our past elected leaders. And if you were me, you might think about how Mary Ann Milner beat me out in the vote to be president of the senior class. I'm not kidding about that last part, but that's just me.

But seriously, by selecting a day to honor our Founding Fathers and other leaders whom we both respect and admire, we can hope to tap their wisdom and their strength and benefit from their trials and tribulations, especially during our own personal challenges. With its focus squarely on older presidents and their achievements, this day also offers us encouragement and hope. When we see how so many of these leaders made it to the most powerful position in the world while overcoming their own series of personal and sometimes (literally) paralyzing setbacks, we realize that we, too, can do anything in this great country we live in.

So, really, Presidents' Day is a time to think about just how hard the job of being president of anything is. Those who rise to that rank are people to be admired, revered, and, if you're really smart, studied. They have accomplished great deeds and feats of strength and courage and, thankfully, two of them were born really close together in February, so we get to think about all of this right after we sleep in on the third Monday of that month.

As with so many of the suggestions carried throughout these pages, the ones described below can be performed anytime throughout the year, whenever you need their particular energies.

- Create your own fantasy board of directors made up of Helpful People and friends whom you admire. These icons can either live with us here or come from other realms, like Gandhi, Bobby Kennedy, Jesus Christ, Franklin Roosevelt, or even Oprah. Whether Abe Lincoln or Martha Stewart, it matters not, as long as you create the bunch you believe can best provide you with the help and advice that you seek. Then, whenever you feel in need, convene a meeting with your fantasy board. Imagine this gathering at night, shortly before you go to sleep. Mastermind with them and then, while you are asleep, the solutions you are seeking to your problems will come to you in your dreams. Keep a bedside notebook handy. The goal of this exercise is to visualize your own band of merry men (and women!) who can create both action and movement for you on the fronts that you've talked to them about.

- Another cure to activate the energies of a George Washington or another Helpful Person in your life is to place his picture in the area that corresponds to this agenda, the lower right-hand sector of home or bedroom. Hang pictures or photos of anyone you believe could be helpful or beneficial to your life in any way. The strength of this cure is carried in the characteristics and qualities (and possibly even the eventual real aid) of any person offering you assistance and thereby making your life immeasurably easier.

• Place an empty glass or crystal bowl here to symbolize your receptivity to beneficial connections. Place the business cards (or pieces of paper with their names or descriptions) of benefactors or even potential benefactors in this bowl. Write preferably in red ink and put down only one name per piece of paper. And, by all means, make sure to clean this bowl out periodically. I simply cannot tell you how many times clients will call me immediately after their appointment and tell me how quickly this one single cure worked. However, five months to five years later they may call and just as quickly complain about their Helpful People energies being in a sort of stall mode. When I ask them when the last time was that they cleaned out the names, business cards, and descriptions of benefactors from their Helpful sector, the answer is usually the same: "The last time you were at my house." It's important to keep this bowl weeded out so that new and better connections are given the opportunity to sprout, strengthen, and grow. And then you will soar to new heights, too, with the help of all your new friends, of course.

MOVING DAY, OR FIRST DAY IN YOUR NEW HOME

About ten years ago, my girlfriend Carolyn and I were sitting in a bar in East Hampton, New York, waiting for my brother Bob (her boyfriend at that time) and his friend Kenny (not mine) to come off a local golf course and meet us for drinks. They were late, and when they finally arrived, they explained that these "two babes" had asked them to have a quick drink at the nineteenth hole, and, well, they decided, as boys are sometimes wont to do, to have a quick drink. In the middle of this whole conversation they were guessing how old their two benefactors were, and when my brother guessed one was in her early thirties, his friend Kenny said, "C'mon, man, did you see her hands? Easy mid-forties. The hands always give it away." I was flabbergasted. Men look at women's hands? And can even guess her age from them? So all the peels and lifts and derma and sheep-pee injections only around the lower-left quadrant of the lower lids didn't matter at all since all the experiences we go through sit squarely on the backs of our hands?

I, of course, immediately looked down at mine and thought, Well, they look like this only because we just moved for the third time in four years, and what with all the packing and the cleaning and the . . . and the . . . STRESS! And there it was! All those big moves (Florida to South Carolina to New York, and then to another place in New York) had taken their toll on me and my hands, and the bell was ringing loud and clear all over the two appendages that hung squarely at the end of my buff-from-carrying-heavy-boxes arms.

Now, keep in mind that during my first two moves, the most my hands ever did was point to the piano and the books, the boxes and pieces of furniture, and even ALL the little-bitty baby stuff. And while I was pointing I was also cautioning big, burly moving men to "Be careful with that, it was my mother's," or "Are you allowed to put those plants over there [pointing to the plants over there] on a moving truck and cross state lines?" (Just in case you're curious, the answer is no. Go ahead and give them away to your friends who will love them just like you did.)

And therein lay this age-old dilemma: Whether you are moving five miles or five thousand; whether you are moving to the house of your dreams or just to make your husband happy because his sister has been taking care of his declining mother for ages and "now it's our turn"; or whether, as is the case in this very navy town that I currently live in, you are moving constantly because you serve your country in a beautiful and honorable way—no matter where or why or when, moving is a big, giant pain in the butt!

And that's just from the packing, boxing, bubble-wrapping perspective. Let's not even go into the promises to be "friends forever" and "never lose touch" part. Then there's the scary and lonely place we go to when we are leaving someplace we have lived, laughed, loved, and planted ourselves in only to have to go and do that all over again somewhere else. I mean, even Patty Hearst wanted to stay with the Symbionese Liberation Army after a while. Even though we all know she didn't leave because she had been kidnapped and brainwashed, I can't help but wonder if she hesitated, just a bit, because she didn't want to pack her sleeping bag and backpack and move on again.

Crying kids who simply cannot imagine leaving their friends and going to new schools. Close friends who know your every secret longing and desire and would do anything to help make them come true. And let's not forget that comfortable feeling of knowing exactly what aisle the Special K is in so that you can just run in and grab the small box because you know the local market like, well, the back of your hand. These and more are explanations I hear over and over and over as to why people dislike moving.

And, as life will have it, quite a bit of my clientele consists of people who have just moved, are thinking about moving, or are in the process of moving. I have empathy. I've done it myself a million times and it never seems to get any easier. The last time, however, I changed my mind and my attitude and began to look at every positive point I could find. See, what I absolutely have come to learn is that we don't always know what's best for us. Moving and meeting new friends and going to new stores and new schools can cause us to grow and become better human beings, even if at first we fight the change like we're fighting the Thrilla in Manila. We can find the best in this anxious situation and make sure our attitude reflects whatever that is. Sometimes old friendships should drop away and our kids will do better in a different school. Sometimes we simply need to trust that the move will lead to bigger and better things and that once we get settled in, we'll love it because we've decided to.

That single statement of commitment makes all the difference in the world. And if we don't or can't get to love the new place, well, then, we'll find another space that fits our hearts, our dreams, and all our taped-up boxes because the pursuit of our own happiness is a birthright promised us from the beginning of time. It's even in the United States Constitution.

And since I have so many clients in the midst of this life-altering transition, I always, as a consultant, try to stay somewhat detached. Because the client who was lying across my lap two years earlier in a state of depression and near catatonia might, at some point soon, become the president of the PTA as well as the "Welcome Wagon Woman" for her block. So I've learned not to get too invested and to do my job to the best of my abilities. But once in a great while a client comes along who engages and invests me in their move and, well, then I go all out. I'll call every day. I'll e-mail every day. I'll get anyone I know in their new area code to lend a hand. Not very professional, but very, very me! This next tale tells of just such a client and will, hopefully, move you to believe that the next time you have to pack up and get out, you'll be armed with all the information you'll need to make the move with ease and grace and abundant expectation. You'll be well armed, in fact, because here it is. I'm here, in this chapter, giving it right to you from the hands I write with, the very same ones I now immerse in Vaseline for fourteen hours every night. But first, as promised, Jackie's story.

She reached out to me during her postdivorce move with her

then-active and emotionally sensitive two-year-old in tow. Talk about stress! I explained to her that one of the keys to moving is to open yourself to the whole process and not get caught up in the minutiae. If a glass breaks, clean it up and move on. It's not the end of the world. More (and really!) important is the directive to give yourself permission to take your time creating your new home. It's not going to happen overnight. Do kitchen and kids' rooms first. I can't say this enough. It saves an enormous amount of anxiety and confusion. Bathrooms and master bedroom come next. All other rooms come after that.

This advice was really important to Jackie (and to a lot of my other clients as well) because they always seem to have specific and detailed agendas all around "the move." But then, once in, they have no plan of what to do inside the new space. They get overwhelmed with confusion, quickly followed by depression. As Jackie was leaving a five-year marriage, separating her son from his father in a full-time way, and moving from a house in the suburbs to a smaller apartment in a city, this move was a tremendously emotionally "packed" experience.

On the day after she and her son moved into their new digs, I told her (and, again, tell all my clients) to find the box with the best wineglasses in it and unpack one. Ditto for a vase. Go for a walk and buy yourself a BIG bunch of fresh-cut flowers. Preferably ones that have a BIG scent attached as well (smell contributes to making great memories). Next, go and buy a good bottle of wine. Go home and put the flowers in the vase, pour and sip some of the wine, and walk around your new HOME in a clockwise direction, giving it love and life and purpose. Room by room. Do this slowly. With intention. Visualize what the rooms will look like when you are finished decorating them, but then give yourself a reasonable timeline to get that done (eight to eighteen months is not unusual). She did all this while giving her little guy his own little sippy cup filled with "celebration milk." They breathed. They visualized. They sighed. And they even cried. They faced their fears and they decided to love their new home. Together. As a team. And they did all that in a few short "celebratory" hours. But they did it before they did anything else.

Jackie told me that that one experience—giving herself permission to unpack according to her schedule and creating a special and sacred moment before bedlam began—transformed a potentially sad and lonely moment into an enriching and hearth-warming one.

Arriving at any new home is filled with a sense of potential and expectation as well as the fear of the unknown. FORTUNE-ately, there are traditions and rituals that help to smooth moves while also giving us advice to part peacefully with the place we used to call "home." We can infuse the new place with positive energy and (one of my favorite words) HOPE. There's only one letter that differentiates those two words, *hope* and *home*. So, as you enter this next stage of your life, welcome it, embrace it, and own it, because, you know, "houses are built, but homes evolve."

YOU SAY GOOD BYE

- Approach your moving day with expectation for new, almost miraculous experiences to occur (here's an affirmation to keep you and the movers company: "All my good flows to me NOW. As one door closes another opens!"), and keep telling yourself that everything, I mean EVERYTHING, happens for a reason and that reason is ALWAYS for your highest good even if it doesn't seem like that at the moment. But before you greet the new home, you need to say goodbye to the old one. This is really a critical part of moving from happiness to ultimate peace in the new place. When leaving your last space, bless it and make a list (write it down!) of nine reasons why you were grateful to live in that space. Even if you moved back to your old bedroom in your parents' house in between college and the first apartment, and while you were home your mother made you keep a curfew again, write down nine blessings you received from that time and then speak them aloud nine times. It's just another way of saying thanks. And then adios!

• As you pack, the MOST CRUCIAL part of moving is to sort through your stuff and get rid of anything you don't need or love. If I were with you, in person, right now while you were moving, I would be screaming this, so I'll say it again here: GET RID OF ANYTHING YOU DON'T NEED and/or LOVE! Please try to remember that every little thing you put around you has an effect and an influence on you, your attitude, your behavior, and all the opportunities out there waiting for you. Great-aunt Edna's rose chintz overstuffed chair might have been just the ticket while you were crashing in the basement of your buddy's house, but do you really want it in the new cool pad? If the answer to that is yes, then take it with you. If you waffle for even two seconds, GET RID OF IT! Sell it or give it away to a shelter or even leave it on the street—someone will pick it up and use it. Just don't bring it with you.

• Here's a "releasing" custom found in almost every ancient tradition that allows you to shut down your connection to your old place, making way to open to all the good stuff in the new one. Envision, in your mind's eye, a cord stemming from your own umbilicus that reaches around the entire old house (or room) in a clockwise direction. Once you can "see" that both you and the previous place are "tied to-gether," imagine that you now hold in your hands a giant pair of scissors. Now cut this cord (sort of that old "Here are the keys to the city" kind of visual) and watch as YOUR part of the cord retreats back into your body. EXHALE as this other imaginary cord then begins to unwind and goes coun-terclockwise around the other space as it disappears through the old front door (or main entryway). This ritual not only readies that space for some new occupants but will allow you to move freely forward without any inhibiting attachments. Cool.

• If you can't quite detach and want to bring a bit of the old place with you (most clients will do this only if they antici-pate that they won't be able to avoid or alleviate "homesick-ness"), carry a small bit of water and soil from the old house to the new and disperse both ONLY around the outside of the new house.

AND I SAY HELLO

• From the MOMENT you officially close on your new HOME, call this space, "my new HOME." Not the new apartment, condo, town house, or house. Not Fort Benning or Iraq or the University of South Florida. HOME! Try never to refer to it in any other way. This will be harder than you think, but will be well worth the effort when you see how your energy will feel so, well, "at home" once you begin to put this advice into practice.

• Create at least one pleasant, comfortable, and "safe" space shortly after you move in. This will be the place you go to when you just cannot unpack one more box or look for one more book or see the earphones without the video iPod attached to it because you have no earthly idea where it is. A chair with a favorite throw on it or even just a favorite painting hung on a wall that will give your soul some solace and sunshine just by looking at it. Or do like Jackie did and put a vase on an empty countertop and keep it filled with a floral reminder that this too shall pass and, in between, you should never forget to stop and smell the roses. To create and celebrate a beautiful image in your new HOME amid the chaos of boxes and bedlam will empower and draw to you health and happiness and prosperity. I promise.

- Mark your territory. This is one of the oldest (think Jimmy Stewart and how he helped the immigrant Martini family acclimate in the movie *It's a Wonderful Life*) yet one of the most worthwhile HOME-warming ceremonies passed down through the generations. Somebody must have known something, as it continues to cleanse and clear and create a happy atmosphere to this day. Place a loaf of French bread, a jug of wine, and a bit of kosher or sea salt in any container that will house them all (generally a basket) and, while carrying them, meander lovingly through every room of the house. Visualize what you think your perfect home would look like, whether or not you have the wherewithal to accomplish everything or anything at this moment. Finish in the kitchen, where you will open the wine, dip the bread first in the salt and then in the wine, and eat, eat, eat to nourish and bless ALL the energies in your new HOME.

- Put brand-new sheets on your bed to signify your brand-new start in this new space and surroundings.

- Even though I know that as you packed, you got rid off all the "stuff" you didn't need, as you unpack, do this process again. Go through your things and your belongings and, once again, give away anything you can't or won't use in your new home.

· Use lots of lighting and lots of music (noise) in those first few days and weeks of moving in. Believe it or not, this will make the place feel more "homey" until it starts to take "you" shape.

· Grab a handful of birdseed (or, really, Cheerios will do) and go outside your home, wherever that is, and feed the local animals. This connects your energies to theirs on an invisible and ethereal level, and they will then become your friends and protectors.

· Buy a brand-spanking-new welcome mat (one that you really, really love) and put it in front of your front door. Put nine coins of any denomination inside a red envelope and place it under the new welcome mat to bring money into the house. The idea behind this is that every single time you come into the house you will, on a subconscious level, KNOW that you put that mat there and that you love it. That show of self-love then translates into the energies you carry into your new HOME with you, and, all of a sudden, home is a happier place to be, especially as you walk into it.

· What you see as soon as you open your eyes in the morning will have an influence and an impact over your whole day. Make sure you love what you see as SOON as you awake— from amber-eyed kitty to your grandmother's antique armoire—it will absolutely influence what happens to you ALL DAY LONG. As a girl, I used to have one of those old ballerina jewelry boxes—you know, the kind that when you open the top of the box, a little plastic ballerina pops up and begins to dance around. Mine played the tune "Oh, What a

Beautiful Morning" from the classic musical *Oklahoma!,* and I began every day with that same sentiment. Even now, I get a beautiful feeling every morning that everything's goin' my way. What you think, say, and see first thing every day creates your very life. Oh, what a beautiful day!

SAINT PATRICK'S DAY

Is this *the* Luckiest Day of the year?

Legend has it that Saint Patrick was known the world over for having driven the snakes from Ireland. We read tales of him standing upon a hill, staff in hand and like some Celtic pied piper, beguiling these serpents into the sea. And while it is true that to this day there are still no snakes in Ireland, chances are pretty slim that there actually ever were any. However, since the symbol of snakes was used prolifically in the pagan religions of old, the idea that Saint Patrick drove the snakes from Ireland was most likely the symbol of his abolishing all pagan practices and driving the Druids (the most magical of ancient religions in Ireland at the time) to practice in places like Glastonbury and Avalon. And, of course, he was sainted by the Catholic Church for the act of bringing Christianity to the Irish people. I guess that was pretty lucky for the Catholic Church.

The Irish and luck have forever been entwined. The Irish revere the clover plant, as its leaves are said to be charmed with the ability to bring us each Health, Happiness, and Prosperity. And according to the oldest legends, Eve carried with her a four-leaf clover when she left the Garden of Eden for good and ever. It's been held in high esteem as a charm ever since, specifically to ward off evil spirits.

The Irish considered the finding of any clover a sign of luck, but finding a four-leaf one brought with it the biggest bang of

Home Blessing Ceremony

Your new home's energies can have quite an impact on you and your loved ones, so it has become standard ritual and routine among many traditions and customs to "bless" the home, or clear it of any unwanted or unnecessary energies and/or visitors. The gold standard of these ceremonies involves cleansing the house's history so that a fresh start can be enjoyed by all the new inhabitants. And please be aware that it is optimal, of course, to bless the house before you move in. But you can, as well, perform this sacred ritual at any time to receive many beautiful and blessed benefits. New Year's Day is an especially effective time to clear and cleanse the house, whether you moved in twenty seconds or twenty years ago. I, personally, perform this ritual every New Year's Day:

• Take the skins off nine oranges or lemons or limes. Pick one of these fruits; don't mix the citrus. I traditionally use orange as the conduit, as according to Feng Shui, oranges are known to lift both spirits and moods. Usually, though, if I'm lifting spirits, I might be inclined to a glass or two, but, like I said, that's just me. Using either lemons or limes is GREAT for addressing any persistent or chronic health issues. Tear the skins into small pieces and put them aside in a container.

• Fill a large glass or crystal bowl with distilled or bottled water (you don't want to use tap water, as it is considered to be "dirty"). Using thumb and forefinger of the hand you write with (considered your "power" hand), pick up the citrus skins, add them to the water, and let them sit and soak for at least twenty minutes.

• Using the same two fingers from the same hand, flick this citrus water all around the new home—on everything—the carpet, the walls, the ceiling, the furniture, the bed, everywhere. Beginning at the front entryway, walk the house in a clockwise direction, finishing back at the front doorway. If there are other levels, go to the second level next, then the basement, then the attic, in that order.

- Next, put some of this same water into an atomizer and go from room to room, in that same clockwise direction, spraying the ceiling corners of each.

- As you do this, visualize that any and all predecessor or negative Chi (energies) are now leaving this space, making way for your new and wonderful opportunities to thrive.

Some last parting advice: I have learned that with any attempt at cleansing a space, your doors and windows should be kept open to give the energies that need to depart a way to get out. No matter the weather, leave something open so that they can scoot.

all. It is traditionally thought that of the four, one leaf is attributed to carrying the qualities of faith, while one holds the harbinger of hope, the third will bring true love, and the fourth is for, what else, LUCK! Irish soldiers have long been known to wear the symbol of the shamrock to stave off death in battle while bringing them fortuitous escapades and escapes, and so began this collective belief that the Irish were a spectacularly lucky bunch. And maybe, just maybe, being Irish was exactly why I was drawn to a vocation that studied fortune and luck from every conceivable angle. And sometimes I feel like that saint of old, with a special mission to drive squiggly, slimy things from your life and then share what I know so you can make every day YOUR lucky day!

It would naturally follow that you don't have to be Irish to be lucky on St. Patrick's Day. In fact, YOU can be lucky every day that comes before the seventeenth of March (the day old Saint Pat passed) and on every one that follows. As mentioned, luck, and the pursuit of it, is a cornerstone of Feng Shui philosophy, with most Feng Shui practices meant to either attract marvelous luck or banish all the different sorts of bad that we might just encounter. Luck is so integral a component of Feng Shui, in fact, that we actually define it in five different types:

1. Heaven Luck: This is where the planets and stars were in the Heavens and the skies on the absolute second that you took your first breath. Rightly so, then, this "luck" focuses on the circumstances of your birth and is readily associated with what we might call your "destiny." For those familiar with astrology, this is the point at which we would say that even though the stars might impel, they cannot compel. Otherwise, where your stars were the second you were born can create a cosmic construction of a sort of starry DNA, but you always and forever have your own free will to override or overcome what the Heavens may have in store for you and your daily existence. According to some practitioners of this modality, this can constitute 40 percent of your personal luck. DESTINY.

2. Man Luck: You know when you walk out the deli door and there's a twenty-dollar bill looking straight up at you from the sidewalk below? You look around and there's no one there who might have dropped this little windfall. You even go back to the coffee counter and ask if anyone's come back hoping to reclaim their money. Nope. It's all yours

now, and based on stories I've heard exactly like this one, you'll probably take a portion of this plenty to play that day's lotto, and then win another five bucks on the scratch-off ticket. Okay, you get it, this is what we call "Man Luck." In a way, your attitudes and expectations can create this sort of luck and these kinds of opportunities. Is your glass ALWAYS half empty or pretty close to full, just needing one more shot? This sort of luck is said to determine roughly 25 percent of yours. CHANCE.

3. Earth Luck: This is the equivalent of the concept behind the Eastern philosophy of Karma, that whatever you do to others will come back in kind to you. It's the Golden Rule. No, not the "be quiet" one, but the one that says to "do unto others as you would have them do unto you." "Love your neighbor as yourself." But in this particular philosophy, whenever you perform a benevolent act, that kindness will return to you three- to tenfold. Twenty percent of your luck is attributed to these personal pay-it-forward actions. KARMA.

4. Knowledge: This luck pertains to your education and your willingness to continually learn and grow throughout the whole of your life. We understand that continual knowledge and cultivation of the self also improves the odds of good and lucky happenings in your life. Fifteen percent of your luck is directly related to what you know, whether or not there's a diploma from Harvard hanging on the wall or one from the school of hard knocks. KNOWLEDGE IS POWER.

5. Feng Shui: This final type of luck is a way of manipulating our environment through harnessing the invisible energies around us in order to support our intentions and manifest our dreams. By enhancing the energies all around us, we

then influence the ones that are inside us as well. Each area of your life can now vibrate with energy and power. Embodied by virtually all the different schools of Feng Shui, it is understood that taking this step to self-empowerment can supersede ALL other kinds of luck that are surrounding you infinitely in the Universe. Using Feng Shui techniques in and around your environment can lift your life from suffering to eventual peace and happiness. Now, that's what I call 100 percent lucky!

MAJOR (AND PROVEN!) FENG SHUI LUCK CURES

1. Paint your front door red or green (preferably red!). The front door symbolizes the "Mouth of Chi"; it is where the fresh, vibrant, happy energy from the outside comes calling to push the old stale stuff away. This door, the main entryway, is, literally, considered the entrance of all opportunities to enhance and improve your life. Just imagine, if the entrance is lucky, well, once inside, so will everything else be. This portal to all things personal impacts your thoughts, your health, your happiness, and your prosperity. Painting your front door red is an age-old and classic Feng Shui adjustment to claiming a better life along with better luck This gets even better. The front door not only is recognized to be the place where the energy enters but also is said to represent what happens inside the entire house. Red is considered the most auspicious color in the Feng Shui pantheon, a harbinger of both fortune and luck and, BONUS, will bring Health, Happiness, and Prosperity to all who live under the roof (and even the loved ones who may have moved away!). If you are looking to improve your fortunes, or even to see a change in them, paint the front door red

and watch and wait as you just know what will come knocking next both loudly and clearly!

2. Change your sheets, change your life. The stats on how much time we spend in our beds change constantly, but, believe me, it's a lot. Your own personal energies, or Chi, can change in many wonder-filled ways if you simply line the linen cabinet with something fresh and different. This is certainly one of the simplest yet most efficient and EASI-EST ways to increase your luck and change your Chi. And if you lived in my family, that had to be done every Sunday morning, before we got ready for church. Shift your relationship energy by buying a new set of pink sheets (if you are still looking for that right relationship). If you're in the relationship but it needs a little vavoom, slip in between red satin and wait for the sizzle. Green sheets are more than for betting on horses; they will bring babies and healing. Purple sheets bring money while you sleep, and blue helps with anything related to studying, learning, or wisdom. As Shakespeare said, "To sleep, perchance to dream." I say, use this bedsheet color-changing cure and there won't be any "chance" involved.

3. Place a red flowering plant, inviting luck, abundance, and prosperity, to the left of the front door (as you look at it from the street). Since this plant will be outside, all appropriate weather concerns should be noted.

4. Hang three Chinese coins (the Good Fortune Coin Cure) on nine or eighteen inches of red ribbon (or string, thread, or yarn) on the inside handle/knob of your front door. Be sure that the yang side (the one with the four characters on it) is facing out.

5. Place a green leafy plant to the left of the kitchen sink. This will alleviate any important or abundant energies from "going down the drain" in that room, most associated with

both health and wealth as well as indicative of a great de of your fortunes and luck.

6. Placing a bamboo plant anywhere inside your living space is said to bring luck and longevity, strength and flexibility, to all your endeavors. Try to have an uneven number of stalks unless otherwise advised or indicated in other adjustments.

7. Hang a metal wind chime directly outside your main entrance to invite the winds of fortune and luck to blow your way.

MORE CUSTOMARY WAYS TO ATTRACT GREAT FORTUNE AND REALLY GOOD LUCK

- It is understood that if you catch a falling leaf you will soon catch some luck as well.

- In the Orient it is believed that the third day of any new moon is a tremendously powerful and really lucky day—a terrific day to create new intentions and bring new and happy, hope-filled realities into your existence.

- While we're talking about the Moon, if you gaze at the new moon holding silver coins in your hands, you will soon find a real boon to your bottom line.

- Wearing a ring on your thumb is considered VERY lucky.

- Remember to try and hold on to the very first coin that comes to you on the very first day of the New Year. It will bring you money all the year long.

- Burning a baby's first diaper is thought to bring a bonanza of luck all his or her life long.

When a Red Door Won't Do

If you share a common space, or, for whatever reason, cannot paint your entire front door, or put a red flowering plant in place, and/or hang a wind chime outside the main entryway, then do the following: Take red nail polish or paint and paint a small circle, at your eye level, on the left side of the doorjamb (again, as you look at it from the street). If possible, paint a small red flower, and you are making the most of a lucky situation! Hang a wind chime directly inside (and I mean right inside) the front door so that the bottom of the chime just ever so slightly grazes the top of the door whenever it opens or closes. Lots of luck in this little tip.

• It is not only good luck to wear blue beads because they are the color of the skies above and bring Heavenly help, but they are also expected to keep evil away. The saying goes, "Touch the blue and the wish will come true." We see brides believing this all the way down the aisle.

• FAST Luck: On any day, add citronella to a bucket of warm water and thoroughly wash your kitchen floor to become awash in FAST fortunes and all things luck.

• RED FAST Luck: Universally recognized to attract FAST fortune and luck. Combine a few drops of the following oils: cinnamon, vanilla, and wintergreen—each is colored gold, but when combined will turn a crimson red. Dab this on money to attract more or on your bedposts to attract some sensual heat. Even dab some on yourself to make sure that day is YOUR Lucky Day.

• Choose any charm that represents an intention, wish, dream, or desire. On any new moon place the charm beside a pink candle and let the candle burn out fully and completely. Attach the charm to a bracelet and wear it to make your wish come true. When this goal is achieved, you may want to do this again with another charm. Pretty soon, you'll not only have a pretty charm bracelet but a pretty perfect life, too. As well as, of course, a lot of burned-out pink candles.

TRAVEL

This single ideal, sector, or area called Travel, in most of my clients' experiences (and homes), is the one space where most of the time I actually need to pull teeth to get them to share their dearest dreams and desires with me. They readily share their desires to find the perfect spouse or lover. They can always use a few more dollars to pay for necessary (and unnecessary) things, and, without question, are more than happy to divulge their dreams about the ways in which they wish to improve their relationships with their kids, their bosses, and/or their neighbors. And they are willing to spill all to me when it comes to their jobs, their money, their health, and their romantic lives, faithfully following through with the cures, customs, and traditions I offer to ensure them a bit of luck and fortune in every one of those areas.

When it comes to traveling, well, they just seem to sit in the backseat, but almost never one on a plane, train, or automobile. Either they can't find the time to travel or just don't believe that there is a place in their environment that can create two tickets to paradise. I tell them if they just put a brochure and a baklava there (lower right-hand space in their home or office), they might soon find themselves cruising the sunny Greek isles. Then

The Luck of the Irish

Here's a great recipe you can combine with some candle Shui to create true Irish luck. The trick here is to keep six green candles burning not only while preparing and serving this dish but also while eating and cleaning up after it as well. The combo of the Irish ingredients along with the magical powers accorded to the burning of the candles will truly make this day especially lucky for all involved!

Irish Cheddar and Guinness Fondue

1/2 cup extra virgin olive oil
1 big bunch fresh broccoli heads, broken into approxi-
   mately 2 cups of florets
1 large cauliflower head, broken into approximately
   2 cups of florets
3 cups halved small red-skinned potatoes
2 pears, cored, seeded, and sliced
1 pound Irish Cheddar cheese, finely grated
2 to 2 1/2 tablespoons all-purpose flour
1 cup (or to taste) Guinness dark stout
6 tablespoons pear juice
3 tablespoons horseradish mustard

1. Preheat the oven to 375 degrees.
2. In a large mixing bowl, drizzle the olive oil over all the vegetables and toss to cover. Place in a roasting pan and cook in the oven for twenty minutes or until browned and tender.

> 3. Arrange roasted vegetables and pears around the edge
>   of a rounded platter.
> 4. Toss cheese and flour together in a large mixing bowl.
> 5. Bring the stout, pear juice, and mustard to a slow
>   simmer in a large saucepan over low heat, gradually
>   adding the cheese mixture and stirring constantly
>   until the cheese is melted and smooth. Add more stout
>   if the cheese mixture needs to be thinned.
> 6. Transfer the fondue to a fondue pot or large bowl and
>   dip in veggies or Irish soda bread (available at most
>   bakeries and markets, especially around Saint Pat's
>   Day!).

I have to hear ALL the reasons they can't go anywhere. The kids, the cat, the money, the plants, the money plant, and on and on and on. And, of course, 9/11. It seems to me that it's far easier for them to believe that lighting those two pink candles in the romance area will have George Clooney moving in on Saturday than to check out their Travel *gua* and give it a go.

The excuses are there and they are real, as are all the different adjustments, or ways, around them. One of my corporate partners (who has now become one of my best friends) has a congenital lung condition that she has to keep a very close eye on. She also has to travel to China every four to five months for her job. She always comes home from these trips East (and I mean always!) with the "Asian flu." You see the pictures of people in the Orient with their Michael Jackson–style surgical masks on, all trying to avoid the myriad pollutants in the Oriental air. Jane, my friend, tells me that spending all the time she has to on a plane for those multihour trips doesn't help either—with passengers coughing and sneezing and none of the window people wanting to bother their aisle mates to step over them to go wash their germ-ridden hands. As a result, it usually takes Jane at least two weeks and a strong antibiotic to get herself back to normal. But it's an integral part of her business and she has to take these trips to take her hefty paycheck to the bank. She wishes there were a magic bullet or a magic carpet (more on that later) to take these trips on but just keeps trying her best to make her efforts easier.

My client Dan has an even stronger excuse for not traveling. He was on one of the planes pulled out of airspace on 9/11. During those years, his sales job was predicated on him traveling back and forth from Boston to Washington, D.C., in order to maintain his livelihood. He has two beautiful children and a wonderful wife. And he truly loves to fly. But after 9/11 he quit his job, and he works from home now. For half the salary. His wife went back to work.

And then, God bless her, there's Lauren. She's watched *Under the Tuscan Sun* about a thousand times now (I know, because I've watched it with her at least half of those), and has all things Italian around her house—everything Italian everywhere BUT in the Travel area. When I ask her why not, ironically, she tells me the same thing: "If only there was a magic carpet." She doesn't like flying, doesn't believe she should tap her savings to go to Italy, and, mostly, she doesn't want to do it alone.

So I often find myself reminding my clients that these energies (cures) work the same way for Travel as they do for all the spaces or arenas of their lives. And then I explain that once you put your Italian intentions into that specific space twenty-seven days prior, you might just have to start packing on Friday to meet George at his villa in Italy over the weekend. I recently had a couple of clients who had tickets to travel on a famous cruise line (if Kathie Lee could see them now), and they were debating whether to cash in and not carry on because of passengers who were sometimes suspiciously disappearing off the sides of these ships. They're back now and they had a great time. But they also were wise enough to bring along Feng Shui as a shipmate.

So whether we are traveling for business or pleasure, we can all use all the luck we can muster to ensure a safe trip without disruption or delay, accident, illness, or injury! Here's what I say to make your trips, your lives, and your dreams tip the travel scales from nervous to not:

FIRST THINGS FIRST:

- Create your own "traveler's luck" and place a picture, post-card, or brochure (that sort of thing) of the place that you are traveling to in the associative area of your living space (once again, this is the lower right-hand sector of the main floor, living room, or office). If you are taking a ski vacation, you might want to leave a set of skis there to symbolize all the luck that will rain down on you as you journey, but my guess is that you might need them. So, just a postcard or a picture will do.

- Prepare your home for your return: Clean the clutter, tidy up, throw out old food that can spoil or expire, empty the trash cans, make the beds, and sort through the magazines and mail.

- Stock your cabinets with some canned foods that will greet you upon your arrival back home. Not only will this sur-round you with the energies of abundance while you are traipsing around the Austrian Alps, but it will also give you something to nibble should you arrive back in your own kitchen later than you thought. The beer in the back of the fridge can accompany your midnight snack of canned tuna and crackers.

• If you have arranged for someone to babysit the plants, the fish, the animals, and especially your kids, please ask her to remove all her belongings from your space prior to your arrival. Also, be sure to remind her that the house should be left in relatively the same condition that she found it in. Take it from me, there is NOTHING worse than arriving home exhausted from a trip only to find five hours of cleaning ahead of you.

• Be sure to check with the hotel(s) that you will be staying at to enlighten them that you don't want to be in any room near a common area or shared space. Hearing a raucous group exiting the elevator well past midnight directly across the hall from your door, or giggling teenagers getting ice from the machine seemingly attached to your headboard, can make a long-awaited vacation a journey into hell. I'm pretty sure they don't let you send postcards from there either.

• Pack a favorite scent or incense or even small fragrant candle that you love. This will allow you to acclimate more easily to all the places you'll go and make you feel more comfy if you are feeling the least bit homesick. I usually bring a small spray bottle with a few drops of lavender essential oil. Just add water and spray the room to clear away anyone else's energies while also promoting calm and serene (and antiviral, antifungal!) spaces!

HAVING THE TIME OF YOUR LIFE

Now that you've arrived, you can have the time of your life!

- Wear or carry a piece of jade with you to protect you from any health issues or concerns while you are traveling. Jade is considered the most precious of gems in all of the East particularly because it can imbue you with a healthy attitude while bringing along the bonus promise of boosting your immune system and adding longevity to your lineage. Keep a small piece in your pocket and touch it frequently, or, better yet, wear it in a piece of protective jewelry that will safeguard your most precious commodity, YOU!

- If you are staying with friends, bring your hosts a gift of fortune and luck. Fresh-cut flowers in an earthenware container that they can put somewhere in the center of their home or kitchen or even dining room will bring them Health, Happiness, and Prosperity. That's better than wine and cheese any day.

- Carry along a small bell to serve several purposes. If you hang this on your hotel or bedroom door you will be immediately alerted should someone enter. Also, ringing the bell nine separate times (or in all the corners of the room you're staying in) will clear out any predecessor energies and give you a good clean space to embark from.

- Retain your Feng Shui protocol. If your energies will flush at home, they can also waste away in the hotel room. Keep all bathroom doors and drains inside the room shut while not in use.

- If you are on (or want to be on) a romantic rendezvous, burn two pink candles in the Relationship area of your room (far

back right-hand corner) to pack just the right amount of al-
lure into your trip.

Follow these directions and ensure that excitement will accompany you on your next excursion!

HONEY, I'M HOME!

There's also some Lucky Shui for when you return home from
your travels:

- Upon your return home, open all the doors and windows
(no matter how briefly) to bring fresh, healthy Chi, or energy, back into your space. Turn up the lighting and the
music and walk the house clockwise to create a new (and
supportive) flow of energy for both you and your home.

- As you reenergize, you can smile, say hello, and bless all your
things as you stroll around. They have missed you as much as
you have (or maybe not so much) missed them. A good affirmation to repeat here is: "I now catch up with my good for
before I called I was answered" (Florence Scovel Shinn).

- Also, as you walk the space, turn on water faucets for a few
seconds to help create a "flow" of Chi; also turn on your
stove's burners, as this will QUICKLY reactivate wealth and
prosperity (money) Chi.

- Try to unpack your luggage in a timely manner. Any time
away from home always gives us a new perspective, almost a
fresh start of sorts. Don't allow those energies to stall by al-
lowing your bags to sit on the floor begging to be emptied.
Unpack and do the laundry, put toiletries away, and so forth,
before the dog does it for you. He tends to hide and gnaw on

new shoes as opposed to putting them back in the closet where they belong.

BUSINESS TRIP

I'd love to say that the majority of my clients just do their Feng Shui then sit comfortably at home as the money and the lovers roll in, all the while planning their next cruise down the Seine (although, truth be told, I do have a few whom that description encapsulates perfectly). Sorry to say, though, it's not the norm.

Occasionally I get called in to consult with the inveterate business traveler whose husband or wife or mother or kids are in constant turmoil about danger or distress lurking around every baggage handler—especially now that we have to watch whether a bottle of mother's milk might actually feed some fanatic's vision of his own one-way ticket to Nirvana. In that case, I share my normal sentiments: "Let it go, because man attracts whatever he fears." I tell them that if the trip is Divinely inspired and worth the efforts, then they should bless it and quit with the resist. What I absolutely KNOW will happen if they are even remotely thinking that the trip will be a bust is that all the plans will burst, and they can expect that—one big bust of a trip.

Many of my clients who phone me with career concerns are sometimes the same ones who travel quite a bit, and so one usually goes hand in suitcase with the other. And although they mostly want to know how to get ahead at their job or even find a way to stop missing their families so much while they are away, they have been bitten by the travel bug and actually like moving around from place to place. They just want to make the traveling part a touch easier. And when they enact these Lucky Shui cures, the trips themselves naturally become more productive and prosperous with the least amount of angst crawling all over

Ellen's Advice from the Shui Archives

- Travel with one nine-inch piece of red string, ribbon, or cloth tied to each individual piece of luggage; this not only makes your bags easier to spot, but my clients swear it brings them up the carousel sooner rather than later. Lucky traveling Shui.

- Before leaving home, placing a picture, symbol, or small statue of a bear in the Helpful People area (lower right-hand sector) is said to keep your home and all its belongings protected from robbery, misfortune, and, really important, fire. Think Smokey!

- Wherever you are, hang a small, round, faceted crystal on nine inches of red string or ribbon (don't forget the tape or thumbtack) directly over where your head lies while sleeping in the bed. This will not only balance the energy of the room but also bring sweet dreams at night and smooth thinking during the day. That's important when you are trying to find out where to catch the next underground to Hamburg from London.

- And just because my friend Karen would kill me if I didn't add this, because she swears by it . . . always enter a plane with your left foot first to guarantee safe footing during all your travels.

them. Luckily, here comes the Shui to scratch that itch, as long as bedbugs aren't involved.

- This might seem obvious, but you would not believe the number of clients I have who thought this was pure genius: Take pictures of your family with you and place them somewhere in your room where you will see them almost immediately upon waking. This really does create and keep up an energetic connection with your loved ones while you are away. There is a codicil here, though. Make sure you can spare the snapshot just in case you mistakenly leave it in the last spot.

- Be sure to take your room key card with you after you leave. Don't hand it back to the clerk behind the check-in counter. Take it home and shred it. Or burn it. Cut it up. But YOU dispose of it. That little key card has EVERY SINGLE PIECE of information that the hotel has about you encoded into it, *including your MasterCard number.* And anyone who works at any hotel or who even knows someone who works at a hotel can find a way to become you while you are in a conference room trying to sell the next better mousetrap.

- If you are Feng Shui–friendly, select a space that already has good Feng Shui. Mr. Trump uses Feng Shui in all of his real estate endeavors—even the hotels. In fact, you'd be surprised (no, really, you would) at how many hotel and motel owners have Feng Shui built into the architecture. So, the next time you're due for a trip, you may want to travel through the cyber first and see if you can select a hotel/motel with good Feng Shui floor plans all set for you to view on the Internet.

- If you have a big meeting or you feel you need some extra validation and support, carry a small conch shell with you. Like the brass-bell technique (ring the bell nine times to clear stale or stagnant predecessor energy in your room as well as ring out your reputation), carrying the conch will bring bright and reputably responsive energies to your endeavors. Way beyond the sea, your reputation will just float along.

• Salt is said to absorb negativity, nervousness, and fear. In fact, in China, the night before her nuptials, the bride-to-be actually might soak her tootsies in salt water (or rice) to get rid of the proverbial cold feet. Grab about six to eight salt packages from the coffee counter in the lobby and pour them into a cup or even an ashtray in your room. Not only will this help to give negativity the shake, but it might just give you a leg up on the competition. Even something as simple as lighting a match and letting it burn out (or a bit more complicated, like lighting a favorite incense) will also absorb negativity and make the space you are temporarily sleeping in all yours.

• Scent a pillowcase with a calming, soothing smell (like lavender or chamomile) and take that with you as you travel from place to place. Little Billy might have to give up his blanket, but Big Bill can carry his pillowcase if it means he'll have a better trip!

• Here comes the secret but really, REALLY effective Shui: When traveling for business and trying to make your very best impression, carry a small red (think tea or birthday) candle with you. Light the red candle in the Fame area (far back wall in the center or middle of the room) of the space before departing to guarantee all your plans will go perfectly. You really will add heat and sizzle to your reputation, and recognition as well. You can either let the candle burn out before you leave the room or just let it stay lit for a few minutes while mustering the courage and the calm to go and get the job done. This works like a CHARM! (When I went to meet with the publishers to sell this book, the Fame area of my hotel room looked like a flaming red-light district.) As with anything fire-related, make sure that everything is COMPLETELY out before leaving your room. It's bad Shui to cause a fire in a hotel, and even worse if you're staying at your sister's house.

- Here's another surefire Shui way to bring in the bucks while you are traveling. Move some receptacle (again, a cup or the hotel ashtray) into the Wealth area (far back left-hand corner of the room as you stand at the door and look at the room as a tic-tac-toe board) and fill it to overflowing with coins. Understand that in many cases that change might be taken as a tip by whoever cleans your room, but don't let that disturb you. Instead, remember that "Whatsoever a man soweth, that shall he also reap." This instant Karma is gonna get you . . . whatever you want while on that trip. And I'm pretty sure you'll get the best chocolate the hotel offers on your pretty-smelling pillowcase, too!

- Last, but certainly not least (in fact, I always do this FIRST), if you know whom you will be meeting with or know the names of the people whom you want to impress or who might want to impress and partner with you, then write their names down. Write them in red pen and place them, one by one, into the Helpful People (lower right-hand corner) of the hotel room. Better yet, if you can somehow get a business card from your potential partner(s) ahead of time, use those influences instead in this corner of the room. This is a secret Shui cure that causes the most unlikely miracles to manifest. Truly!

LABOR DAY SHUI (OR ANOTHER REALLY "FUN!" WEEKEND IN THE CAR!)

Traveling anywhere on a daily basis usually involves not only us but also our motorized best friends, our well-oiled, gas-gulping spoiled outer appendages, better known as our cars. Let's face it, with the cost of sky travel skyrocketing and more of us traveling on vacation by car, we should know the basics of backseat Shui to save the driving day.

And speaking of the backseat: "Are we there yet?" becomes so much less intense fingernails-on-the-chalkboard when your daughter is surfing her Sudoku book looking for the next challenge to complete, as opposed to ripping the corners from those same pages, making spitballs, and flicking them at the little screecher sitting exactly to the right of her.

Whether it's the daily commute, a holiday drive over the river and through the woods, or the first three-day weekend in September to mark the end of another spectacular summer, the time spent in our cars should be smooth and peaceful and only add to a totally trippy travel experience—expect anything else and you should just gas up the grill and stay home instead.

Fast car, or slow minivan, or first car in high school (Ford Falcon), there is a way to bring peace and prosperity to our drive time and it's called Feng Che (distant driving cousin to its more worldly, well-known relative, Feng Shui). Feng Che (wind and vehicle, respectively) can make an opportunity to get you to where you are going with Health and Happiness and Harmony, the three *H*s that, in raw reality, can definitely beat out the double arches.

Our cars definitely reflect our personalities right along with our peccadilloes. In fact, unless you have plenty of public transport available, you probably spend as much time in your car as you do in almost any other space in your life (at least that's what the studies say!). So Car Shui isn't as much about your commute or time spent driving as it is about making all the highways and byways in EVERY aspect of your life more empowered and power-full, from the cushions to the carburetor and every detour in between.

And, just like its Feng Shui (wind and water) cousin, Car Shui has some dictates of its own that will help keep any negatiⁿ ergy that's driving to the beach next to you in its own lane, making you the Yoda of lane hoppers, Road Sage. Following any of the next suggestions means never having to say you're sorry to the wife, the kids, the dog, or any other drivers on the mean streets, and, fortunately, vice versa.

- Never leave clutter in the car, which includes candy wrappers, fast-food bags, sucked-dry Starbucks cups, or cracked CD covers. You should treat this space as you would your home and readily realize that clutter contributes to drive-by negativity.

- It's especially essential that the center of the vehicle remain clean and clear. This space relates to the health not only of the driver but of all the passengers as well, which should be enough of a reason to pull over the minivan and pull out the Mini-Vac. The energies here should be smooth and flowing, like your ride.

- Adding ten drops of lemon essential oil to a spray bottle filled with distilled water and spritzing the inside of the car will help those obvious odors caused by mildewy wet towels that never made it from beach to the clothesline, while bringing a bright, sunshiny scent to your driving experience.

- Play soft, soothing music during the ride, no matter the urge to rock out. Tunes that are simple in melody and flow will provide peace after the hour-long fight to listen to head-banging blast . . . Bad Shui!

- Hang a small, round, faceted quartz crystal on a red string from your rearview mirror. This will pump positive energies inside the car while additionally fueling a circle of protection around you and all those you're traveling with.

- Speaking of protection, it's paramount in Car Shui to make sure that all mirrors, inside and out, are kept completely clean as well as in perfect positions to put you in that same space. You can even affix a convex mirror to the back bumper of your car to deflect any negativity that's ready to sideswipe all your intentions.

- Last, keep a few extra and comfy cushions in the car to keep everyone feeling safe, secure, and protected—these are especially useful for the littler passengers and usually make the trip go smoothly.

	9	
Wealth and Prosperity	Fame and Reputation	Relationship, Romance, and Marriage
Family, Friends, and Ancestors	Health	Children and Creativity
Knowledge and Self-Cultivation	Career	Helpful People and Travel

IT'S NOW TIME for me to echo what my thoughtful, wonderful Irish "Gran" used to say (and most likely one or two of your grandmothers as well) when I replay the standard caution shared with the four kids in my family (in the middle of winter when we were running out to play in the snow with our favorite board shorts and hoodies on): "What good is all the money in the world, or all the love your heart can hold [that word was really played up for good and guilty measure] if you don't have your health? Now put on your mittens and zip up those hoods!"

Well, really, what good is that stellar job with the corner office and the name on the door, the great grades, all the fabulous family adventures, or, okay, I'll say it, "all the money in the world" if you don't have your health? That's why this single space in your home is so vital, so instrumental, and so important. It's considered the "heart" of the home as it is located in the direct center of your space, just like your own beating organ is inside your own beautiful self. And since this energy does sit dead center, it also touches all the other energies that we have been addressing to make our lives more wondrous, more miraculous, more positive, productive, and prosperous.

Think about it, this single sector touches every other energy on the map, in our homes, and in our hearts. It's as if all the other energies are the blood that circulates to our heart, bringing our center a rush of nourishment, only to have the heart push out all the debris that might keep us from our fullest happiness, harmony, and health. The Health area represents our health on every conceivable level—physical, mental, emotional, and spiritual, and as such it needs to be nurtured and nourished just as our bodies, minds, and psyches do.

Its location, as I stated above, is the center of your home, office, or any other room in which you spend your precious time. Its element is earth and the colors are both brown (grounding, center-ing) and yellow (stimulation from the Sun). So we put fresh flow-ers or healthy green plants in ceramic or terra-cotta vases here as they all represent and come from the earth, and they all symbol-ize our intention to stay as healthy as possible for as long as pos-sible in as many ways as possible. Because, after all, you can have everything, but if you don't have your . . . oh, you get it!

The number accorded to this central area is the number 5, so a great way to fold in applicable accessories to your decor while ac-tivating these health-inspiring energies is to add five big, juicy, healthy lemons (in an earth-friendly container like a wooden bowl or woven basket) to the center of your home. If this doesn't work, put the citrus in the center of either your dining room or kitchen table; it can never hurt to try to always have a bunch of fresh-cut florals placed here in the Health area as well, representing beauti-ful Chi imbuing everyone with your own healthy endeavors.

TAKING A SICK DAY

The guy in the cubicle next to you has been sneezing his germs your way for four-plus days now. And, speaking of plus, two kids with strep plus two kids with strep equals four kids with strep, all at school, all surrounding your own sweet angel, who soon enough will have that gigantic cotton swab heading down his throat, too. Or what about that gal in seat 9a who just coughed her way through your entire flight to Philly? But since you fac-tored in your sick days to add to your last vacation, you simply and absolutely cannot and will not ("Achoo" . . . God bless you) GET SICK!

Even though I KNOW we have the ability and all the infor-mation necessary to heal our own bodies, sometimes we cannot help what's coming from the food handler who just delivered our chicken quesadilla. However, if we consciously and regularly take measures to maintain a healthy state of mind as well as a healthy state of being, then we can boost, bolster, and resist whatever is causing little Johnny to scratch and scratch and scratch like that. By the way, can't he go home and do that?

The following (sometimes literal) cures offer you the power to heal yourself. They work if you feel something coming on, if it's already on, or even if you've only just learned about them as you're rounding the bend from sickness. And if used with belief, faith, and trust, then that bend you round won't be on your way to an open all-night pharmacy.

Here we go:

- Carry any piece of jade with you or wear jade jewelry. It's important, especially if you are ill, that this gem comes in pretty constant contact with your skin. Jade is considered by most Eastern traditions to be the jewel of longevity and has been known to possess near-miraculous and healing powers and properties.

- Place a red sheet between the mattress and the box spring of your bed. This will stimulate your immune system and help to heal you from the inside out.

- Sleep on yellow, green, or blue sheets. They conjure healing from a colorful space. In fact, unless you are a single woman looking for a mate and sick and tired of that search (in which case you should just go for it and paint your room pink or salmon), ALL bedrooms should have a propensity of greens and blues in them. There's a reason they use those specific colors in hospitals.

- If you are very ill it is often advised that the walls of the bedroom should be painted white, as this color is considered to hold within it all the colors of the rainbow, making it intensely and powerfully healing.

· Diffuse lavender essential oil around your sick space. This serves as a holistic antibiotic, antibacterial, and all-around antisickness very special cure. Put a bowl of steaming water somewhere in your room and add six to ten drops of 100 percent pure lavender essential oil. If you are congested or all stuffed up, you can also add an additional six drops of either tea tree or eucalyptus oil to the lavender and then open up all the way to wellness.

· Hang a SIX-ROD METAL wind chime to the side of your bed—preferably the side that you sleep on. It must have SIX rods to have the health and healing effect we're after here.

· Drink GREEN TEA. Every day. At least one cup. Every day. Drink green tea.

· This cure is applicable only if you are really, really sick, recovering, or recuperating. Put nine or eleven live, healthy green plants inside the room that you sleep in. For the same effect, put a bamboo plant with five stalks in any bathroom that relates to the room where you slumber.

· Put white flowers in a blue vase immediately inside the front entryway. This is considered the cornerstone of all cures for kidney-related ailments, but is also widely reputed to help with healing on all levels. Get rid of the bouquet and replace it with a fresh bunch as soon as the flowers begin to wilt or you will, too.

· Keep the area outside your main or front door brightly lit at all times while you are feeling low. This will lift your energy and help to replenish weak Chi.

- It bears repeating because this cure works so well in getting you well that to place either five or, even better, nine fresh, healthy lemons in a wooden bowl and put it somewhere near the center of the home (the Health area) aids and affects health and healing for everyone who lives under that roof. And remember to get rid of those fruits as soon as they begin to wilt!

OH, MY ACHING BACK!

The single most common physical complaint that I consistently hear from clients is about back pain—back pain that extends to the neck, the shoulders, the lower back, sciatica, scapular, well, you get it, and chances are either you or someone you know has it.

Of course, there are many tried-and-true methods of ameliorating this annoyance. You can see the chiropractor, the physical therapist, the osteopath, the masseuse, or any or all of the above. Or you can try the following cures:

- Get any natural container (NOT plastic!) and fill it with a tiny bit of uncooked rice.

- Then place nine pieces of white chalk (yes, like the kind you used to do math problems with on the board in fifth grade) on top of the rice in the container. Hey, are you smarter than a fifth grader? I'm telling you, this really works.

- Last, place this bowl under your bed directly under where your back pain is. Leave it there for at least nine days. You should see a reduction in the pain in a fraction of the time. Now, there's a lesson you didn't learn before the bell rang.

SCALPEL, PLEASE . . . LET'S CUT OUT THE CONCERNS AND GET ALL BETTER

Nothing, absolutely nothing, in my practice grabs my attention like a client who calls with concerns for a loved one who is ill and needs an operation. Most of them are hoping that I will offer some quick cures (and I mean that in the literal sense of the word) to prevent their beloved patient from having to go under the knife. At the very least they want some reassurance from me that there is a way to work some magical healing energies to give their guy or their girl, mom, or dad, or even their child, an energetic advantage while under anesthesia.

I can't help but become fully, 1,000 percent, engaged when someone's health (and obviously happiness) is at stake. Like Kelly, who called me because her eighty-year-old mom was having her hip replaced and she wanted me to come to the hospital and activate her room with healing energies. It appeared she would be recuperating there for quite a while. Or like when my best friend phoned because her youngest son was possibly going to be born breech and needed to be delivered by cesarean section. Then there was my client Danny, who was having a knee replaced but also needed to know that he could continue to participate in triathlons once the staples that were holding the new joint in place were removed and he had an okay from his doc to run (bike and swim) free.

Story after surgical story, all anybody ever really wants is some sort of reassurance or guarantee that their life will return to normal as soon as possible, and that maybe, just maybe, this Feng Shui stuff could get them over the stiff, the stuck, the nausea, and the nurses just a bit sooner than even that.

Although we all know there are NO guarantees in life, here goes my best cure for "Operation Day" (and the recovery time that follows); it's not foolproof, but not foolhardy either. I've never not seen a tremendous result from following this advice. And coming from me, who has been doing this for almost fifteen years, that speaks volumes:

- Healthy green plants bring healthy green (or healing) Chi to any room, but they are especially effective in a hospital room. They are said to ensure a safe operation with a bonus side effect of enhancing a speedy recovery. So in the patient's hospital room (this can work in either YOUR or THEIR bedroom as well, but in my experience not with as strong results) place nine small plants in a line that runs from the door of the room to the patient's bed. If because of logistics that's not possible, then line up the same number of plants on any windowsill in that room. All the while, everyone involved with this exercise should be visualizing a complication-free surgery with a miraculously speedy recovery.

- Once the patient has been moved, either to her own home or maybe even to a rehab facility, this nine-plant cure can be enacted all over again. But do not bring the plants from the hospital room home (or to rehab) with you. Leave them for the next patient or to be disposed of by the hospital staff as they see fit. This is really good Karma for you and a really easy operation for them!

THE HEART WANTS WHAT THE HEART WANTS

There is an ancient Shamanic custom to do a certain visualization when any organ is in trouble to bring complete health back to that organ, and therefore to the body as a whole. It says that you should go within (in your mind) and find the diseased or sick part of the body and then tell it that you love it and *watch* (visualize) as it smiles back at you. You can imagine how well that little piece of advice goes over with some of my clients. But I share it just the same because I think it is so sweet and I love it, love it, like I love my own body parts, especially when the last laugh's on them.

The Feng Shui method mentioned here to help heal a heart is in NO WAY intended to take the place of any modern allopathic medical advice on how to care for one's most vital organ. But these cures are old, old, old, and, again, I have had clients who have used this advice to great success, BUT ONLY after I made them promise to go see their cardiologist. Believe me, if nothing else, that doctor will get a smile on his or her face when you tell him about this next cure. It's entirely up to you to make your heart smile, too.

THE HEART CURE

Put nine ice cubes into a white pot. The pot MUST be white so that the ice then takes on that same hue and appears to be white as well. Add one tablespoon of camphor to the ice in the pot. (You can usually get camphor at any pharmacy or even at some hardware stores. If all else fails, there's always the Internet.) Place the white pot with the ice and the camphor under your bed and make sure that it rests directly under where your heart is while you are sleeping at night. And don't forget, right before you go to sleep, to tell your heart that you love it and wait for it to smile back at you. If you do this, we'll all have the last laugh.

EASTER (AND, KINDA, SORTA, PASSOVER AND PURIM, TOO!)

Easter has not only become a singular celebration but has almost assumed an entire season unto itself. It symbolizes a time of rebirth and resurrection, with stories of miracles maintaining a stronghold during these early vestiges of spring. Long before bunnies and baskets were the symbols du jour, spring celebrations and festivals welcoming this season of renewal were established traditions.

The early Saxons prayed to their goddess Eostre (sound familiar?), who represented all things new and natural coming out of a long winter. The Jewish festival of Purim celebrates spring and has as its heroine the good Queen Esther (sound familiar?). During this special time of the year, the Romans and the Christians adopted and appropriated this same theme and attached their own prophet who could walk on water and raise the dead. Not to be *passed over,* Judaica also has its own place in this pantheon of renewal and rebirth.

Renewal, rebirth, resurrection.

Some cures or adjustments hold so much power in them that they can actually begin to act even before they are put into place. Even sometimes just by reading them! Red Egg Rebirth is just such a cure. This one single exercise can purge and make everything anew for you, even addressing some of those deep, dark, and painful parts of your past that you haven't thought about since Christ hung on the cross.

The last time I offered this cure to a client she began to cry on the phone before I even finished the instructions. On some level, well, really, on EVERY level, she was finally ready to shed the past and release herself to a traumatic incident that she had long since buried in her psyche but that was holding her hostage nonetheless. Ostensibly, Melissa called me just to talk about ways to jolt the Chi in her house to get a new job. What she didn't expect was the lightning bolt of remembrance that rocked her world.

In describing her living space to me it was clear that there were issues outside the color of her dining room walls. I could just tell (because it is part of my job, after all) that there was something much darker and much deeper that was creating conflict in her current agendas. We needed to get to that root, but, without a periodontist and a lot of Novocain, trying to cross this canal can often get really messy as well as tremendously painful.

When I suggested to her that I was actually intuiting a trauma from her past that was keeping her from moving into her fabulous future and that she had chosen a house where the architecture suggested this same thing, she let down, let go, and spontaneously remembered being sexually molested as a young child. I immediately understood that this was the real reason she had contacted me in the first place. "It was my grandfather," she whispered, "and it started happening when I was about four years old and continued until he died when I just turned seven." And here she was, approaching forty and still hadn't forgiven or been able to move on from something she barely even remembered. Yet clearly her energies were still held squarely in the clutches of those dread-filled experiences.

And even though I believe in the tremendous healing power of forgiveness, I didn't think that she was quite ready to release the power these incidents held over her own life. But I knew she would eventually be able to forgive. I knew that, with time, she would come to a place where she would realize that forgiving her grandfather's heinous and horrible betrayal and behavior would free them both and allow her spirit to once again trust, take flight, and soar.

So here is the Red Egg Rebirth Cure, a wondrous adjustment that brings about renewal, regeneration, rebirth, and resurrection. Make sure you read through the entire sequence one time fully before beginning your own empowerment.

Enough said. Here's the cure. It's in two stages. Okay, maybe not enough said, just one more time for good measure . . . read the entire sequence through before beginning this cure.

Stage 1

1. It's best to enact this cure between the hours of eleven AM and one PM, but anytime when you can be alone will do.
2. Go and buy a new carton of fresh eggs. Don't let anyone see them once they are bought. This secrecy underscores the highly personal nature of this cure. It has to be about you solely. This can be tricky, as it was for Melissa, whose husband works at home, mother lives downstairs, and five-year-old child runs in and out.
3. For the most immediate results, boil the eggs as soon as you can after their purchase. Let no one disturb you. While the eggs are boiling, visualize all negative energy/sadness, or whatever possible "bad luck" is holding you back, leaving your body, your head, your heart, and your soul.
4. While the eggs are still boiling, in the palm of the hand that you write with, mix one teaspoon of any red spice with as many drops of 151-proof rum that equal your age plus one (so, if like Melissa you are forty years old, you would mix the spice with forty-one drops of rum). Traditionally, the red spice should be cinnabar, which is not exactly easy to find since it is toxic and contains banned mercury. And since I believe the intent is as important as the action, you can use *any* red spice, such as paprika. You can also go to a Chinese store and find a wide selection of bottles with red spice in them and grab one of them. When you begin to add the rum to the spice in your hand, I strongly suggest using a dropper. Otherwise, you might end up starting your rummy count all over again if an errant drop or two jumps the bottle. Mix the rum with the spice using the middle finger of your opposite hand.

5. Now take only *one* hard-boiled egg (you can make a nice egg salad with the other eleven) and roll it around in your power palm until it's covered with the red spice, then place it on a napkin. Then rub your palms together until they are dry. They will be a rusty red. Once again, during the entirety of this cure, be sure to visualize all bad Chi leaving you through the palms of your hands. Only now does good, vibrant, healthy Chi remain.

Stage 2

1. Carry that *one* egg that you rolled in red spice and placed on a napkin somewhere outdoors. Crack the egg very lightly and gently peel off the rust-colored shell, keeping all the pieces of the shell on the napkin. As you do this, envision these pieces as your own old wounds being shed from inside and out—you are shedding disease, negativity, sadness, anger, and any energies holding you back and blocking new, healthy Chi.

2. As you are shelling, visualize the new, perfect, unblemished egg in the womb: This is you, your original pure self, untouched by any illness, conflict, injury, or negativity.

3. You can now consider yourself revived and reborn.

4. Now you have to eat part of the yolk and part of the egg white: If you can't stomach this, that's fine; imagine you are doing so.

5. Then throw the rest of the egg to the four cardinal directions—north, south, east, west. Imagine that the egg is now nourishing the bad Chi that had previously been feeding on you. When it gets full and satisfied, it will go away.

6. Crush the eggshells and throw them as well in the four cardinal directions, imagining that you are finally through with what had been causing you pain, challenge, heartbreak, or any other obstacle to your greatest self-fulfillment.

The Red Egg Rebirth Cure is a very potent and very secret cure used to expel bad luck and ill Chi, so that it's replaced by good luck and positive fortunes. At its deepest level, this symbolizes a spiritual rebirth. You can purge yourself of all sadness and negativity so you can start anew.

The Red Egg Rebirth Cure is my homage to Easter, Passover, and the hundreds of other religious and pagan rituals that come in the spring. In spring, we welcome the rebirth of nature. Out of winter's short, dark, and colder days emerges new growth—and new hope. Our world's religions mark and echo this revitalization in various ways. With Easter, Christians celebrate the resurrection of Christ and the promise of eternal life. With Passover, Jews celebrate God's mercy in sparing (or protecting) them as they fled Egypt.

I can't emphasize enough the power of the Red Egg Rebirth Cure—its power to purge old thoughts, painful memories, whatever in your life you are ready to let go of. So take this opportunity—now at Easter, at Passover, or at any time in your life when you feel ready to release yourself from pain, trauma, or simply bad feelings that you no longer wish to carry with you. And let it go. Scatter your sorrow to the wind and feel the fresh breath of spring waiting to watch your next stages of positive, beautiful metamorphosis.

CANCER

As I don't believe that ANYTHING that occurs on this planet (or on any of the others, for that matter) happens by accident, I also don't think that it is any accident that this is the last Lucky Shui cure that I am writing for this book. I didn't intentionally save it for last. It just sort of organically evolved that way. I wanted to address "grave" or what could be considered "terminal" illnesses, particularly cancer, but I was concerned that it felt too negative and I wanted my book to be joyful, uplifting, and celebratory. I mean, this IS mainly a book about how to make special occasions, events, and celebrations more wonderful. I do offer cures that help us dive into challenges head-on and help ourselves to a new, healthy perspective on what we might normally perceive as something far less than positive for ourselves or for our loved ones on specific or particular days. But cancer? That's so very dark, deep, pervasive, and, sad to say, personal.

I realized that I have so many friends and family and clients who have to live with this illness EVERY single solitary day that I would be remiss if I didn't offer some way to support ourselves and our loved ones facing this or any other grave illness.

If you are presently facing a health challenge on a chronic or even daily basis, know that the information I am about to offer is both potent and powerful, and I have the success stories to prove it. Not in lieu of seeing a specialist but fighting right alongside whatever else is prescribed for your healing and your health, I have seen these cures, time and again, turn people's lives around and restore them to profound places of peace. I say profound because I also believe, at the very core of my being, that each and every illness, disease, accident, or injury gives us a chance to review our own lives while also offering an opportunity to find the blessings hidden within. These are indeed bold words when your hair is falling out and you can't even swallow a Tic Tac. But they are true words just the same.

Ultimately, I suppose, I saved this "energy" for last because I KNOW that if you practice any of the adjustments offered herein, this one WILL NOT be the last thing that you do. Maybe because I didn't know anything about any of this until almost all of my own family, including both my parents, had passed from one or another terminal illness, cancer included. Or maybe because I have witnessed countless people take their health into their own hands and watched them become whole and blessed beings once again. Or maybe, just maybe, because you will see that when you're in dire straits, these cures really do work. Let me share a story.

Last year, my client Pam told me her sister had been diagnosed with stage four (terminal) breast cancer and was given six months to a year to live. Pam wanted to know if there was anything she could do "covertly" because, as she said, "Frankly, my sister thinks Feng Shui or any alternative/holistic medicine is just bs." Like so many other patients, Pam's sister chose to place her faith in chemo and radiation, and her health in everybody else's hands but her own.

So with Pam, the emissary, I ran down the standard laundry list that addresses terminal illnesses: Check electromagnetic frequencies in the house (was she sleeping with her head close to an alarm clock with BIG LCD numbers that were emitting BIGGER EMFs all around her as she slept?). Were all the plumbing, drains, and ducts in the house operating properly (as they represent our own internal goings-on)? Was her bedroom over a garage or her stove in the dead center of her house (both bad Shui), or was there a bathroom directly over her front entryway?

Next I told Pam the things she could do ("covertly" or not) to help heal her sister's situation. She could add or raise the wattage of all the lighting in her house. With everything else going on, I doubted Pam's sister would notice the lightbulbs had been changed, but she would definitely notice that her Chi had. I then told Pam to assess and then fix any damaged plumbing, electricity, or appliances that were draining away precious energies. And, last, I gave Pam the top of the line of all the Health antidotes: Hang a round and faceted clear quartz crystal on nine inches of red string from the ceiling in the center of her sister's bedroom. She could actually also get away with doing this, as there was a ceiling fan stationed there; Pam just changed the pull that came with the fan to a crystal one.

Pam followed through on all these adjustments, and, lo and behold, what do you think happened? Right. I got a call six weeks later that the tumor was shrinking and her sister was getting better, and Pam confessed to her covert activities and her sister was willing to meet with me to talk further. I'll save the assessment of the house for another time, because, in the big scheme, it was more important that Helen (the getting-better sister) learn this next cure, and then practice it with regularity to ensure that her healing energies kept heading in the right direction.

The cure is called the Six True Colors Cure, and I quote from his Holiness and my Feng Shui master, Professor Lin Yun, who says, "To augment and reinforce appropriate medical treatment for this disease [cancer] of abnormal cells, the patient looks at the Six True Colors, transmitting their auspicious color sequence to the afflicted cells."

This Six True Colors system uses white, red, yellow, green, blue, and black (in that sequential order) along with your own positive beliefs, visuals, and healing intentions to restore balance and harmony to the body. I have found that the most effective way for patients to take advantage of the enormously powerful benefits accorded to this cure is for them to make something that transmits these colors to their bodies from something made by their own hands. I have had clients who made rainbows with colored pencils on paper to those who actually crafted a work of art using colored cathedral glass. I even had one client whose mother was in a coma, so she cut strips of colored construction paper, brought them to the nursing home with a big bottle of Elmer's glue, and gently guided her mom's hand over the glued-on color-over-color strips in order to have her mother be the one to have created this medicine. And even though patients are supposed to place this colorful collage somewhere visible so they can meditate twenty minutes each day on it, taking in the color sequence to the afflicted cells, my client still believed that her mother could benefit from this miraculous cure even from behind tightly closed eyes.

I always tell people who are really sick that if they do only one thing to try to get whole, it should be this one. Use the Six True Colors Cure and then allow the energies to do the healing rest. I have seen patients who were set to stay in rehab for six or seven weeks after hip replacements use this cure and get back to their normal lives in as few as three weeks. I have seen premature babies thrive under the light of this cure. And I saw Helen, Pam's sister, just recently at an Avon-sponsored 10K Walk for the Cure. Helen, Pam, and their other sister, Sue, were all walking together three years after Helen's initial dire diagnosis, with Helen leading the family pack, in remission and currently cancer-free.

ACKNOWLEDGMENTS

Whenever I think of all the people and the places and the things that it took to bring this book out of my head and my heart and onto the page, well, I think to myself, "What a wonderful world."

Many thanks and blessings to all the teachers along the way, too many to mention on this single page, who have shared their wisdom, their knowledge, the truths, and their expertise with me so that I might shake them all together and offer them here, inside these pages. And to all of the readers who use even one smidgeon of the luck-bearing traditions contained herein, my gratitude and thanks to you for making our planet a more beautiful and harmonious place to be!

This road hasn't always been easy to travel and so to every person who believed in me and in my passion and in some tangible way has helped me to share this information with the world, from the depths of my soul I am profoundly grateful. That includes Kathleen Burrows, Sarah Whisman and Madeline Couton, my angels Frankie Carl and Jeff Karr, Darden Chronister, Paul Schmidt and Carolyn Beauchamp, Taunia and Dave Reed, Wayne Zinn, Dorothy Barrie, Andrea and Vin Lupo, Tina Merritt, Jeanne Allen, Jon Tutelo, Marie Siani, Cathy Lewis, Susan and the Johnson boys, David and Breda Drury, Grayson Whitehurst and my little sister Christine Shaw, as well as my mentor and big brother, Bob Drury, ALL my gratitude and thanks all-ways!

To the teams of professionals who have illuminated my path so I can shed some light on life, without any single one of you, I never would have been here, so, May God Bless You ALL: Stacy Morrison at *Redbook* and Betsy Berg at William Morris; Joy

Behar; Karen Gerwin and everyone at Creative Culture; Maggie Hamilton; Christina Duffy, Brian McLendon, Cindy Murray, Avideh Bashirrad and Jane von Mehren at Random House; Patty Gift, Ron Schmidt, Lara Stark, Mr. John Willcox, the wise and wonderful Mark Graham, Linda Kelly, and Christina Michelle, all from iVillage; and, oh, did I mention Stacy Morrison of *Redbook?* Lastly, but certainly not leastly, the inimitable Kirk Schroder. Karma kids, Karma!

To all the friends who stepped in and mothered (and fathered!) my son as I strove to complete this manuscript and to the ones who I can always count on to help me share the Shui, thanks, I love you, too! That list includes Auntie Linda, Kim, Jackie and Roger Pierce and Payton and Carter, too. Special thanks to Karen and Mark Stewart, Eileen and Richard Smith and Carole Brighton and Eric Smith. As well to Lisa and Tammy Dodson, Dina Harris, Becky Glynn Accolla, Leslie Law, Beth Von Scoyack, Karen Goodall, Jerelyn Lawrence (Team Kendall), and everyone else who gave of their time and their energies when I was running low on my own, May ALL your wishes in ALL ways come true!

ELLEN WHITEHURST is a leading Feng Shui expert and holistic practitioner. Her unique brand of Feng Shui, "Lucky Day Shui," is based on her more than twenty years of training and expertise in Feng Shui, Aromatherapy, and other modes of holistic healing. She writes a monthly column for *Redbook* magazine, "Shuistrology," which combines the principles of Astrology and Feng Shui. She is also the expert contributor in her field for iVillage.com and contributes to *Natural Health* and *Woman's World* magazines. Whitehurst is a regular and popular guest on many nationally syndicated radio shows.

Her Lucky Day products have been featured in such mainstream arenas as Nordstrom Department stores, Barnes and Noble booksellers, Trump National Golf Courses, and Starbucks, to name a few.

Whitehurst has worked in private practice for over fifteen years, conducts seminars and speaking engagements across the country, and advises thousands who visit her online through her website, www.ellenwhitehurst.com.